Addison-Wesley
Science

Authors

Charles Barman, Ed.D.
Associate Professor of Science Education
Indiana University, Indianapolis

Michael DiSpezio, M.A.
Science Department Chairman
Cape Cod Academy, Massachusetts

Vallie Guthrie, Ph.D.
Director, Greensboro Area Math
and Science Education Center
North Carolina Agricultural and Technical
State University

Michael B. Leyden, Ed.D.
Professor of Education
Eastern Illinois University

Sheryl Mercier, M.A.
Elementary Science Specialist
Fresno Unified School District,
California

Karen Ostlund, Ph.D.
Associate Professor of Education
Southwest Texas State University

Reading Consultant

Bonnie Armbruster, Ph.D.
Associate Professor
Center for the Study of Reading and
Department of Elementary and Early
Childhood Education
University of Illinois

▲▼ Addison-Wesley Publishing Company

Menlo Park, California • Reading, Massachusetts • New York
Don Mills, Ontario • Wokingham, England • Amsterdam • Bonn
Sydney • Singapore • Tokyo • Madrid • Bogotá • Santiago • San Juan

Content Consultants

Thomas H. Callen II, Ph.D.
Program Resource Manager
Albert Einstein Planetarium
National Air and Space Museum
Smithsonian Institution

Jym Ganahl
Chief Meteorologist
WCMH-TV, Columbus, Ohio

Edwin Harper, Ph.D.
Associate Professor of Biochemistry
Indiana University School of Medicine

Robert W. Hinds, Ph.D.
Professor of Geology
Slippery Rock University, Pennsylvania

Chelcie Liu, Ph.D.
Physics Instructor
City College of San Francisco

Luis A. Martinez-Perez, Ph.D.
Associate Professor of Science Education
Florida International University

Linda Medleau, D.V.M., M.S.
Assistant Professor
Department of Small Animal Medicine
University of Georgia

Larry K. Pickering, M.D.
Professor of Pediatrics and Director of
Pediatric Infectious Diseases
University of Texas Medical School at Houston

Linda Sanford
Curator of Youth Education
Morton Arboretum, Lisle, Illinois

Lydia Young, Ph.D.
Senior Engineer
Perkin-Elmer Electron Beam Technology
Hayward, California

Critical Thinking Consultant
Robert Swartz, Ph.D.
Director of Critical and Creative Thinking Program
University of Massachusetts, Boston

Safety Consultant
Jay A. Young, Ph.D.
Chemical Consultant
Silver Spring, Maryland

Testing Consultant
David P. Butts, Ph.D.
Aderhold Distinguished Professor
College of Education
University of Georgia

Cover Photographs: Elephant seals
Front Cover Photograph: © Art Wolfe
Back Cover Photograph: Wayne Lynch/DRK Photo

ISBN 0-201-25420-4

CDEFGHIJKL-VH-892109

Getting to Know
Addison-Wesley Science

This book was written to help you learn science. There are 21 lessons to help you read and think about science and to do science activities.

When you see it means there is something for you to do. When you come to a ✓ you can check what you have learned. When you see ? you will find a question that students just like you have asked. A scientist has answered the question. And when you see 🤖 you will learn about some of the ways that people use science.

We hope you will enjoy learning science.

Contents

What Is Science?

People have always asked questions about the world: How does a plant grow? What do animals need in order to live? How can we predict the weather? Scientists have found answers to these questions. That information is part of science.

There are other questions that do not have answers yet. Scientists are trying to find answers. A special way of finding answers is part of science, too.

Scientists look and listen carefully. They use their senses. But sometimes our senses can fool us. So scientists measure things. They write down what they find out. They test things many times.

Reading About Science

Before scientists try to answer a question, they read. They learn what other scientists have found out. You can learn by reading, too. The information in your science book comes from the work of many scientists.

When you read a science book, read carefully. Find out the meaning of the words in **dark type**. Use the pictures to help you learn.

Thinking About Science

You will find many new ideas when you study science. Some ideas will be easy to understand. Other ideas will be difficult.

Think carefully about each idea. If you do not understand it, ask questions.

Do not give up if you cannot understand at first. Some ideas take time to learn.

Doing Science Activities

When you do activities, you can learn the way a scientist does. You can use your senses. You can write down what you see. You can measure.

Before you begin an activity, read all the directions. Then try to guess what will happen. At the end, think about what happened. Then answer the questions.

Safety in Science

Scientists are careful when they work. You need to be careful, too.

Read all the directions before you begin an activity. Do each step in order. Never smell or taste things unless your teacher tells you it is safe. Be careful when you see a yellow diamond (◊). Clean up when you are done.

Be careful!

Sharp!

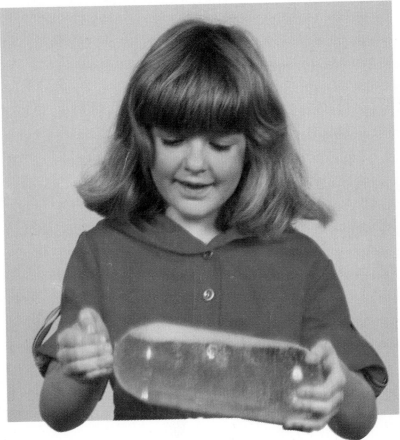

Unit One
Life Science

Life science is about living things. Animals are living things. Plants are living things, too.

In this unit, you will learn about dinosaurs and other animals. You will also learn about plants that make seeds.

Lesson 1
Dinosaurs

Getting Started

Looking at Bones

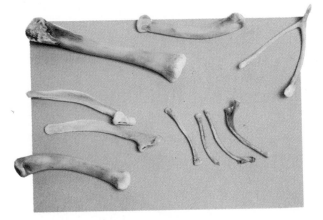

1. Get some bones.

2. Look at the bones. Are they big or little? Was the animal big or little?

3. Take one bone. Guess what part of the animal it is from. Give a reason for your guess.

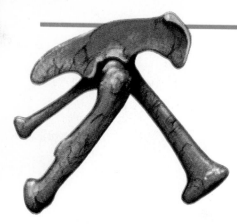

Dinosaurs are land animals that lived millions of years ago. There were no people then. No person has ever seen a living dinosaur. But people have found dinosaur **fossils**. Fossils are traces of animals and plants that lived long ago.

Some fossils are bones, teeth, and footprints that have turned into rock. Scientists dig up the bones and teeth. They measure the footprints. They study the fossils in order to learn about dinosaurs.

Apatosaurus   Deinonychus   Compsognathus

Scientists put fossil bones together. This shows us how big dinosaurs were. Look at the picture. The first dinosaur was as long as two buses. The second one was about as tall as a person. The third one was as small as a chicken.

Fossil teeth show what dinosaurs ate.
Some dinosaurs had large, sharp teeth.
They ate animals.

Tyrannosaurus

Some dinosaurs had flat teeth. They
ate plants.

Iguanodon

Other dinosaurs did not have any
teeth. They ate plants and tiny animals.

Gallimimus

Fossils show how dinosaurs walked.
Some walked on four legs. Some walked
on two legs.

Allosaurus

Brachiosaurus

Some dinosaurs had spikes. Other
dinosaurs had horns. These things
helped keep the dinosaurs safe.

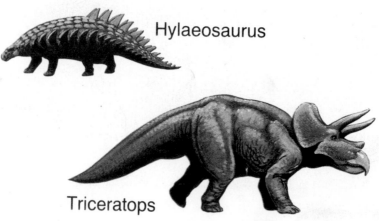

Hylaeosaurus

Triceratops

It is not easy to put dinosaur bones together. The dinosaur in the picture had bones on its back. These bones are called plates. Scientists thought that the plates grew in two rows.

Stegosaurus (old idea)

Now some scientists think there was only one row.

Stegosaurus (new idea)

Can we ever be sure of what dinosaurs looked like?

 # Finding Out

Use these things:
foil pan
plaster of Paris
apron
plastic spoon
shell or leaf
fossil print

Find out how to make a print.

1. Stir the plaster of Paris a little bit with the spoon.

2. Put the leaf or shell on top of the plaster. Do not push it under the plaster.

3. Let the plaster get hard. Take the leaf or shell away.

4. Compare your print to a fossil print or to a picture of a fossil print.

How is your print like a fossil?

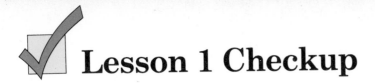
1. What made each of these fossils?

2. What are two ways that these dinosaurs were different from each other?

3. Think! How do animals of today help scientists study dinosaurs?

Lesson 2
The Land of the Dinosaurs

Getting Started

Measuring the Length of a Dinosaur

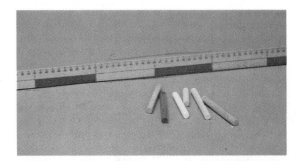

1. Use a meter stick and chalk. Pretend there is a dinosaur on the playground!

2. Some dinosaurs were 20 meters long. Measure 20 meters. Draw a line.

3. Stand on the line with your classmates. Find out how many children could stand next to a large dinosaur.

25

The picture shows how the earth looked when the dinosaurs were living. It was a good home for the dinosaurs. It was warm and wet.

Allosaurus

Ornitholestes

There were many kinds of plants.
The dinosaurs that ate plants had a lot
of food. The dinosaurs that ate meat
had a lot of food, too. They ate the plant
eaters.

Barosaurus

Stegosaurus

Camptosaurus

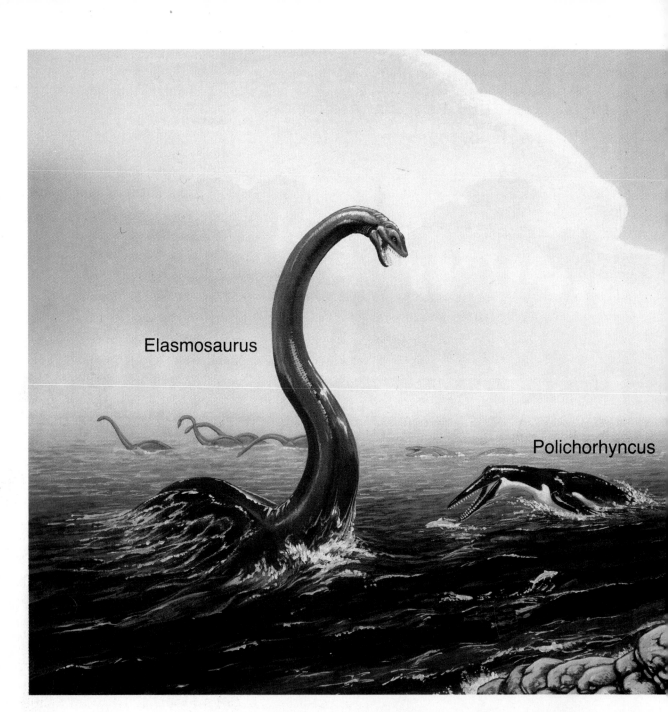

Elasmosaurus

Polichorhyncus

Other animals shared the world of
the dinosaurs. There were swimming
animals and there were flying animals.

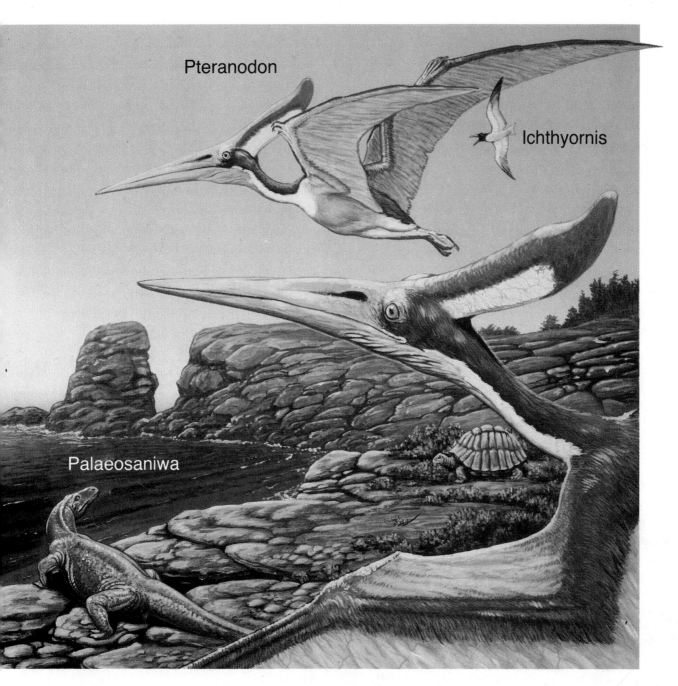

Pteranodon

Ichthyornis

Palaeosaniwa

There were other land animals, too.
The warm, wet land was a good home
for many kinds of animals.

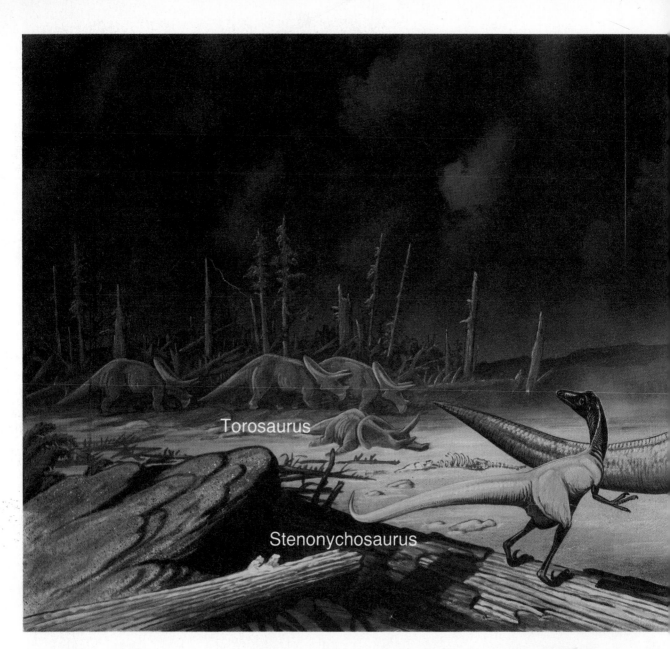

Torosaurus

Stenonychosaurus

There were dinosaurs on the earth for a very long time. Then the world changed. Some scientists think it became dark and cold. Many plants died. The dinosaurs no longer had the things they needed.

Tyrannosaurus

All the dinosaurs died. Many other
kinds of animals died, too. When all of
one kind of animal dies, we say it is
extinct. The dinosaurs became extinct.
There are no more dinosaurs on earth.

Finding Out

Use these things:
shoe box
colored paper
crayons
scissors
tape
clay

Make a model of the world of the dinosaurs.

1. Use the colored paper to make the land and water.

2. Make some plants that lived at the same time as the dinosaurs.

3. Cut off one side of the box.

4. Tape the land, water, and plants to the inside of the box.

5. Make some dinosaurs out of clay. Put them in your model.

How does each part of your model help the dinosaurs?

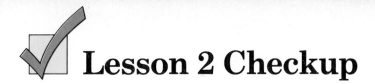

Lesson 2 Checkup

1. Which of these animals are dinosaurs?

2. Which things do not belong in the world of the dinosaurs?

3. Think! If all the cows on a farm die, should we say cows are extinct? Why or why not?

Lesson 3
Animals in Danger

Getting Started

Finding Homes for Animals

1. Use pictures of animals and pictures of places where animals live.

2. Choose an animal. Find a place where it could live. Find a place where it could not live.

3. Think about what the animal needs. Tell why it could live in one place but not in the other place.

All animals need food, water, and a place to live. All animals need to be safe. If an animal's home changes, it may not get the things it needs.

Places change in many ways. Sometimes there are fires or floods.

People change the land, too. Forests are cut down. Swamps are filled in with soil. People make farms, cities, and towns.

How has the land in the picture changed? What happened to the animals that lived there?

Many animals are extinct. Some are extinct because their homes were destroyed. Others could not get enough food or water. Some are extinct because hunters killed too many of them.

The animals in the pictures are extinct. Like the dinosaurs, they no longer live on the earth.

elephant bird

saber-toothed cat

Utah Lake sculpin

Steller's sea cow

Florida manatee

bald eagle

Galapagos tortoise

The animals in the pictures on this page are in danger. There are very few of each kind. They may become extinct. We say that they are **endangered**.

There are many, many endangered animals. There are laws to keep endangered animals safe. But sometimes it is too late to save an animal.

The panda is an endangered animal. Pandas live in the forests of China. Long ago, the forests were large. Pandas could find lots of food. Today, the forests are smaller. People have cut down trees. Farms divide the forests. The pandas have less space. They also have less food.

Pandas eat a plant called bamboo.
One kind of bamboo has been dying.
Pandas cannot find other kinds of
bamboo in the small forests. Many
pandas have died because they did
not have enough bamboo to eat.

People are trying to help. They are
planting many kinds of bamboo in the
forests. If there is enough food, the
panda may not become extinct.

Finding Out

Use these things:
drawing paper
crayons

Pretend to discover an animal.

1. Pretend that you have discovered an animal. Prepare a newspaper story about it.

2. Draw a picture of your animal. Show how big it is. Show what kind of covering it has.

3. Write about your animal. Tell where it lives. Tell what it eats. Tell what else it needs.

4. Show your newspaper story to your class.

Tell about your animal. What does it need to keep from being endangered?

 **Lesson 3 Checkup**

1. Which animals in the pictures are extinct? Which are endangered?

2. What can cause animals to become endangered?

3. Think! How can plants become endangered or extinct?

43

Lesson 4
Seed Plants

Getting Started

Learning About Seeds

1. Use many different kinds of seeds.

2. Sort the seeds by size. Put all the seeds that are the same size together.

3. Now sort the seeds by color.

4. Find another way to sort the seeds. Write down all the ways you sorted them.

The plants in the pictures are **seed plants**. They grow from seeds. They make new seeds.

Seeds can be large or small. Walnut seeds are large. Cactus seeds are very small.

Seeds come in many shapes. What shapes do the seeds in the pictures have?

A plant that makes seeds is a **parent plant**. Some seeds will grow into new plants. If a seed grows, the new plant will be the same kind as the parent plant. For example, a pine seed will become a pine tree. Someday it will be a parent plant, too.

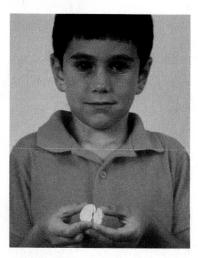

Each seed has a tough outside part called the **seed coat**. If you soak some kinds of seeds, you can remove the seed coat. Then you can open the seed. Inside, there is a tiny new plant. And there is stored food for the plant. The seed coat has kept the new plant safe.

When the plant starts to grow, it will use the stored food. Some seeds have more stored food than other seeds. The seeds in the pictures have a lot of stored food.

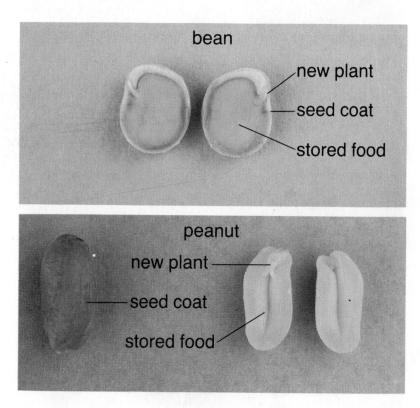

bean
new plant
seed coat
stored food

peanut
new plant
seed coat
stored food

A seed needs three things before the
new plant inside it can start to grow. It
needs air, water, and warmth.

Most seeds are planted in the spring.
It is warm in the spring. And there is
usually enough water in the soil.

The picture shows how a new plant grows from a seed. The small plant is called a **seedling**. It looks like its parent plant, but it is smaller and weaker.

As a seedling grows, it uses up all
the food that was stored in the seed.
After that, it must make its food. Seed
plants can make their food if they have
water, air, warmth, and light.

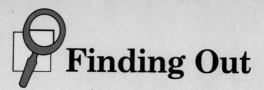 **Finding Out**

Use these things:
seeds
paper cups
soil
water
spoon

Find out what seeds need to start growing.

1. Write "cold" on one cup. Write "warm" on the other cup. Put soil in both cups.

2. Plant three seeds in each cup. Put about four spoonfuls of water in each cup.

3. Put the cup labeled "warm" in a warm, dark place.

4. Put the other cup in a cold, dark place.

Which seeds started to grow? Why?

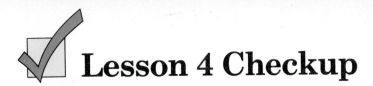

Lesson 4 Checkup

1. What order should the pictures be in?

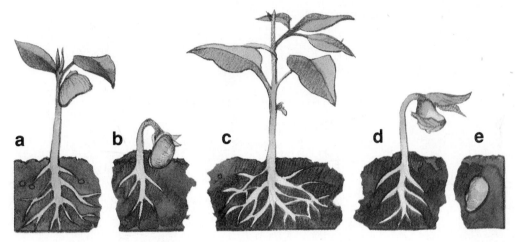

a   b   c   d   e

2. Name each part of the seed.

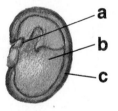

a

b

c

3. Think! Can a seedling grow in a dark closet? Why or why not?

Lesson 5
Roots, Stems, and Leaves

Getting Started

Looking at Roots, Stems, and Leaves

1. Use three different kinds of plants. Each plant should have roots, stems, and leaves.

2. Look at the roots of the plants. Think about how they are alike and how they are different.

3. Draw the roots of the three plants.

4. Do steps 2 and 3 with the stems and leaves.

Most plants have roots, stems, and leaves. These parts look different on different plants.

Each part helps the plant in special ways. All of the parts working together help the plant live and grow.

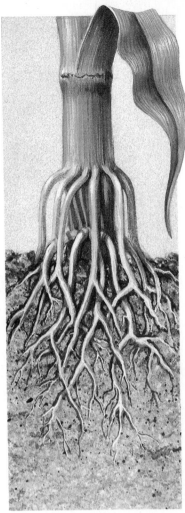

You may not see the roots of a plant. They usually grow down into the soil. Some roots grow deep into the soil. Others grow near the surface. A few plants have roots that grow above the soil.

Roots hold the plant in the soil. They bring water from the soil into the plant.

Stems can be tall or short. They can be thick or thin. They can be hard or soft.

Stems help a plant in several ways. They hold leaves up to the light. They carry water between the roots and the leaves. They also carry food from the leaves to other parts of the plant.

Leaves have many shapes and sizes. They make food for the plant. Leaves need air and water to make food. There are tiny holes on the bottom of a leaf. Air goes in through these holes. The roots and stem bring water to the leaves. Leaves also need light to make food. They cannot make food in the dark.

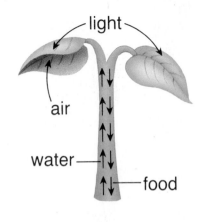

Plants use the food that is made in the leaves to live and grow. Some food is used right away. Other food is stored.

Some plants store food in the leaves. Some store food in the stem. Others store food in the roots. Look at the pictures. In what part of each plant is food stored?

food

food

food

Much of our food comes from plant parts. We eat leaves, stems, and roots of plants. When we eat these plant parts, we are eating the stored food that the plant has made for itself.

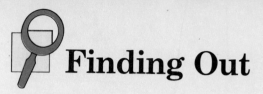 **Finding Out**

Use these things:
white flower
jar
water
food coloring

Find out how water moves in stems.

1. Put food coloring in the water.

2. Put the flower in the water.

3. Wait a few hours.

What happened to the flower petals?

Why did it happen?

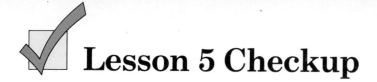

Lesson 5 Checkup

1. I bring water into the plant. What am I? What else can I do?

2. I make food for the plant. What am I? What else can I do?

3. I hold up the leaves of the plant. What am I? What else can I do?

4. **Think!** Which part of each of these plants stores food?

Lesson 6
Flowers, Fruits, and Cones

Getting Started

Learning About Flowers

1. Get some flowers or some big pictures of flowers.

2. Study the flowers. Find different shapes. Find different colors.

3. Look inside the flowers. Look for different parts.

4. Draw pictures of some of the flowers. Find out their names. Write the names on your drawing.

Most seed plants have flowers. Some flowers have bright **petals**. Petals can be many colors and shapes. Flowers with bright petals often have a sweet smell.

Some flowers are small and hard to see. You may not notice them at all. Each kind of plant has its own kind of flower. Compare the flowers in the pictures.

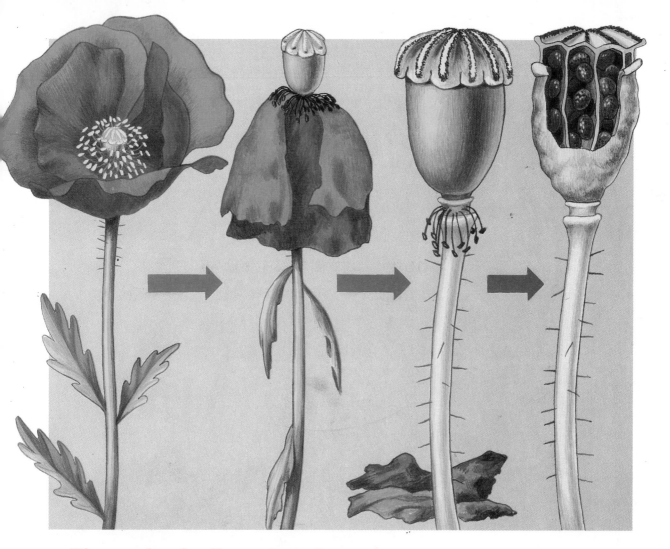

The seeds of a flowering plant are made inside the flowers. After the seeds are made, the flowers change. The petals dry up. They fall from the plant.

The part of the flower that holds the seeds starts to grow bigger. This part becomes the fruit. The fruit keeps the seeds safe.

The pictures show some fruits that we eat. Do some of these pictures surprise you? Many foods that we call vegetables are really fruits. Fruits come from flowers. They have seeds inside them.

Some fruits hold many seeds. Other fruits have only one seed.

spruce

Douglas fir

pine

Some seed plants do not have flowers and fruit. They have **cones**. The seeds are made inside the cones. The cones keep the seeds safe until the seeds are ready to grow. Then the cones open and the seeds fall out.

69

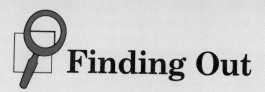

Use these things:
fruits
spoon
graph paper

Find out how many seeds are in some fruits.

1. Take all the seeds out of one fruit.

2. Count the seeds. Write down the number of seeds.

3. Do steps 1 and 2 for the other fruits.

4. Make a graph. Show the number of seeds in each fruit.

Which fruit had the most seeds?

Which had the least?

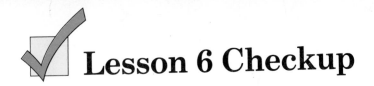 **Lesson 6 Checkup**

1. Match each picture to one of the words.

fruit   cone   flower

2. Look at the fruits. What would each one look like cut in half? Draw pictures to show your answers.

3. Think! Which plant will have fruit?

Lesson 7
Seeds Travel

Getting Started

Learning How the Wind Carries Seeds

1. Get a strip of paper, scissors, and a paper clip.

2. Fold the paper in half the long way. Then open it up.

3. Make two wings. The picture shows how. Then put the paper clip on the bottom.

4. Drop the paper. Watch the way it moves.

Most plants make many seeds.
Some plants make millions of seeds
in their lifetime. The seeds must leave
the parent plant before they can grow.
Some seeds will grow close to the parent
plant.

Other seeds must move away from
the parent plant. There might not be
enough space for many new plants.
There might not be enough water. New
plants that grow under the parent plant
might not get enough light.

Seeds have different ways of moving. Some seeds are carried by the wind. These seeds are not very heavy. Many of them are fuzzy at one end. The fuzzy part is like a parachute. Other seeds have wings. It is easy for the wind to carry these two kinds of seeds.

Look at the seeds in the pictures. How do their shapes help the wind carry them?

Some seeds have hooks. The hooks catch in the fur of animals. Sometimes they catch on people's clothing. Animals and people can carry the seeds far away from the parent plant. These seeds are called "hitchhikers."

Some seeds pop out of the parent plant. When the fruit gets dry, it opens suddenly. The seeds shoot out. They travel a short distance from the parent plant.

Other seeds are carried by water. These seeds will not sink. They can float far from the parent plant.

Some seeds travel to places where they can grow. But many travel to places where they cannot grow. Seeds may fall in places where there is no soil or water or warmth. Many seeds are eaten. What else could happen to seeds?

Some plants make many seeds. Only a few of the seeds will find a place to grow into new plants.

Finding Out

Use these things:
different seeds
water
pan
cloth

Find out how some seeds travel.

1. Blow to see which seeds can travel with the wind.

2. Find out which seeds can float.

3. Find out which seeds can hitchhike on fur or clothing.

How can each seed travel?

Can any seeds travel in more than one way?

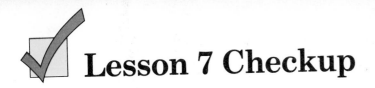

Lesson 7 Checkup

1. How does each seed travel?

2. Which seeds have a good place to grow?

3. **Think!** What would happen if all seeds grew into plants?

Technology Today

Two Plants in One

Most plants have only one kind of fruit. But what if someone wanted more than one kind of fruit on a plant? They would need to join two plants. This is called **grafting**.

Look at the picture. It shows two kinds of pears on one tree. Two kinds of pear trees have been grafted together.

You could graft two kinds of apple trees together, too. You could even graft an orange tree to a lemon tree!

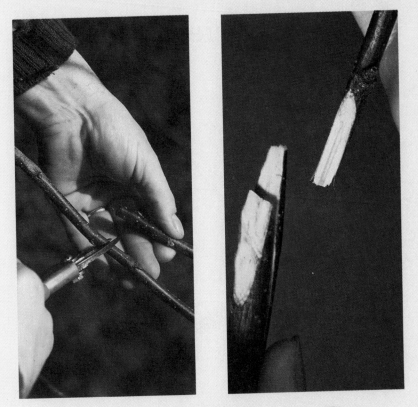 

Here is how grafting is done. First, most of a branch is cut off a tree. A slit is made in the part of the branch that is left. Then a small branch called a twig is put into the slit. Last, the twig is tied in place.

If the grafting works, two kinds of fruit will be on one tree.

Think About It

Why would people want to grow two kinds of fruit on one tree?

How can you tell what kind of animal a fossil used to be?

Mr. Rodie's class
Virginia Court Elementary School   Aurora, Colorado

Dr. Winans is a scientist who studies fossils. She is called a **paleontologist**. Part of her job is helping people learn about fossils they have found.

When someone brings Dr. Winans a fossil bone, she first looks at its size and shape. If it curves a certain way, she might say it is a jawbone. But how can she tell what animal it is from? To find out, Dr. Winans would compare it to other jawbones.

The bottom jawbones of many birds are pointed in front. They have no teeth. And none are as large as some dinosaur jawbones. Dinosaur jawbones are not pointed. Most have teeth. Fish jawbones can be large or small. They are made up of many bones.

By comparing fossils in this way, Dr. Winans can tell what kind of animal a fossil came from.

bird jawbone

dinosaur jawbone

fish jawbone

Melissa Winans

85

Unit Two
Physical Science

Physical science is about things in the world around us. It is also about how things can be moved or changed. We can know about things in the world by using our five senses and by measuring.

In this unit, you will learn some ways to measure things. You will learn about magnets. You will also learn about light and shadow.

Lesson 8
Matter

Getting Started

Learning That Things Take Up Space

1. Use a clear plastic cup, water, three rocks of different sizes, string, tape, and a crayon.

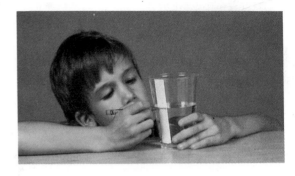

2. Fill the cup halfway with water. Use tape and the crayon to mark where the top of the water is.

3. Tape a piece of string to the smallest rock. Put the rock into the water. Mark where the top of the water is now.

4. Do step 3 again with the other rocks. Compare the marks for each rock. Think about why the marks are different.

Water, rocks, and other nonliving things take up space. Plants and animals take up space, too. Look at the pictures. Is there anything in the pictures that does not take up space?

Things that take up space are called **matter**. The amount of space that matter takes up is called **volume**. Which things in the pictures have more volume than others?

Things that take up space have **mass**.
Mass is the amount of matter that
something has. If something has a large
mass, it feels heavy. If it has a small
mass, it feels light.

In the picture, Bob is carrying a box
of clothes. Chip is carrying a box of
books. The boxes have the same volume,
but the box of books is heavier. The books
have more mass than the clothes have.

Some matter is **invisible**. It cannot be seen. Air is invisible matter. Air does not seem to take up space or have mass, but it does.

In the picture, Crystal's toy has air in it. Luis's toy does not. Crystal's toy has more volume than the other toy. The air inside it takes up space.

Which toy do you think has more mass? How could the children find out?

In the picture, the children are playing a game. When the music stops, they must sit down. There are six children. There are only five chairs. What will happen?

People are matter. They take up space. Each child will take up space in a chair. If something takes up space, nothing else can be in the same space at the same time.

Matter can be put into three groups. These groups are called **states of matter**. The first state of matter is **solid**. A solid has its own shape. A solid does not change shape when it is moved from place to place. Look at the pictures. The radio has the same shape in all places.

The second state of matter is **liquid**. A liquid does not have its own shape. It takes the shape of its container.

A liquid can change shape, but it always has the same volume. A small volume of liquid will not fill a large container. A large volume of liquid cannot fit into a small container.

The third state of matter is **gas**. Most gases are invisible. Air is made up of gases.

A gas can change shape. It takes the shape of its container. When you put air into a tire, the air takes the shape of the tire.

The volume of a gas can change, too. If a tire gets a hole in it, some of the air will spread outside the tire. That air will take up more space.

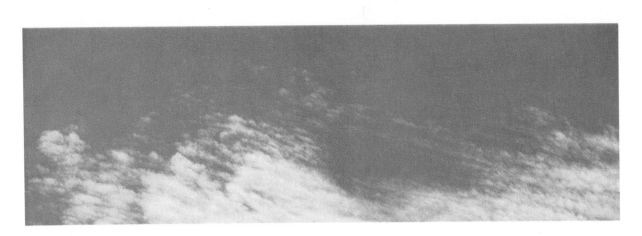

There are many different kinds of matter. Look at the pictures. Tell the state of matter of each thing. Tell if it is living or nonliving. Tell if it can be seen or if it is invisible.

Now tell how the things in the pictures are alike.

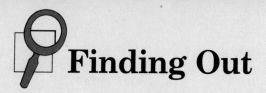 **Finding Out**

Use these things:
paper
cup
pan of water

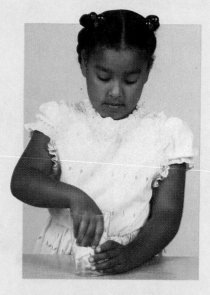

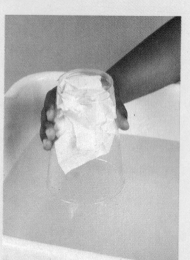

Find out if air takes up space.

1. Wrinkle up a piece of paper. Push it into the bottom of the cup.

2. Turn the cup upside down. Make sure the paper will not fall out.

3. Put the cup into the water upside down.

4. Lift the cup out of the water. Look at the paper.

Did the paper get wet?

Why or why not?

Lesson 8 Checkup

1. Which thing in each pair has more volume? Which has more mass?

2. If one thing has more volume than another, does it also have more mass?

3. **Think!** Name each thing in the fish tank and tell its state of matter.

Lesson 9
Matter Changes

Getting Started

Changing Ice to Water

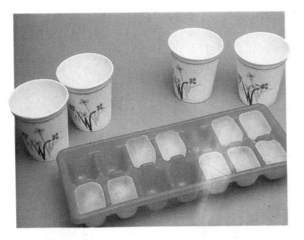

1. Use ice cubes that are in paper cups.

2. Put the cups in different places around the room.

3. Predict which ice cube will melt first. Write down what you think.

4. Check the cups every ten minutes. Find out if your prediction was right.

Matter can be solid, liquid, or gas. These are states of matter. Matter can change from one state to another.

A liquid can change to a solid. Water is liquid matter. It can **freeze** and become ice. Ice is a solid.

A solid can change to a liquid. Ice can **melt** and change to water.

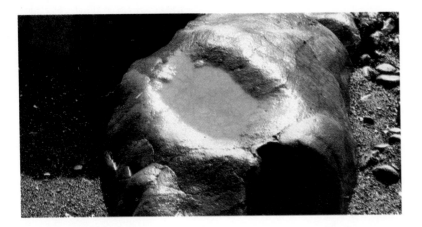

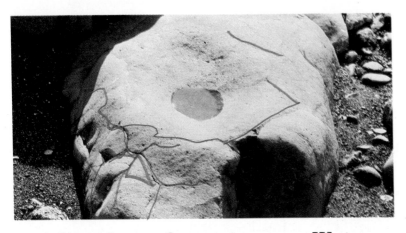

A liquid can change to a gas. Water can change to an invisible gas called **water vapor**. Water vapor can spread into the air. When a puddle dries up, the water turns into water vapor.

A gas can change to a liquid. Water vapor can change to drops of water. The drops of water in the picture are called dew. Dew comes from water vapor in the air.

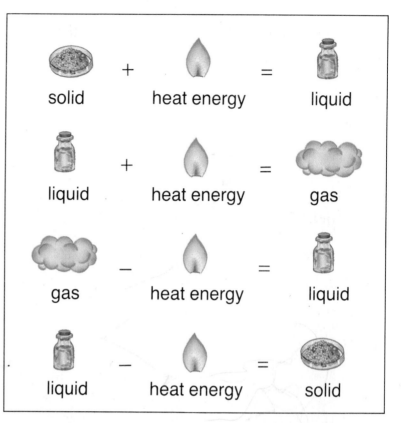

The chart shows why matter changes state. Heat energy is added or taken away.

What is happening in the pictures at the bottom of the page?

Almost all matter can change state.
But some things must get very hot or
very cold before they can change.
Usually, you see these changes for only
a few kinds of matter.

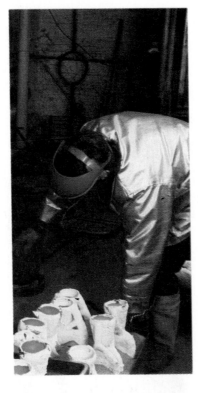

Finding Out

Use these things:
clear plastic cup
ice cubes
cold water
food coloring
white napkin

Find out how water changes from a gas to a liquid.

1. Fill the cup with water and ice cubes. Add two drops of food coloring.

2. Wait until there are drops of water on the outside of the cup.

3. Wipe the outside of the cup with the napkin. Find out if the water has any color.

Where did the water on the outside of the cup come from?

How do you know?

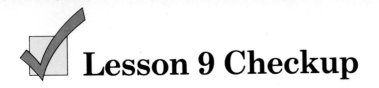

Lesson 9 Checkup

1. What change of state does each pair of pictures show?

A

B

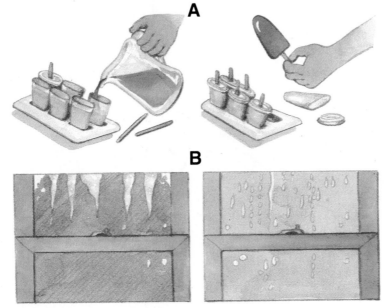

2. What caused each change in the pictures above?

3. Think! What happens to the water when wet clothes dry?

Lesson 10
Measuring Matter

 **Getting Started**

Measuring Heights

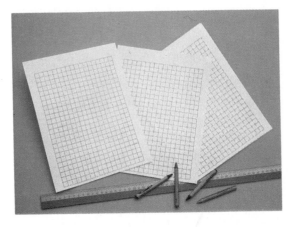

1. Use a meter stick, graph paper, and crayons.

2. Measure the height of all the students in your class.

3. Make a bar graph of all the heights. Each student can color in a bar for his or her height.

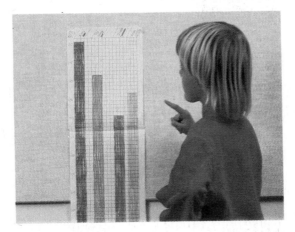

4. Use the bar graph. Find out who is the tallest. Find out if any students are the same height.

1 centimeter
(1 cm)

The girl in the pictures wants to know which plant is taller. In the first picture, she is comparing the plants to each other. In the second picture, she is measuring the height of the plants.

When you measure, you compare something to a unit. When you measure height or length, you can use units called **centimeters**. A centimeter is a **standard unit**. Every centimeter is exactly the same size.

25 meters

45 meters

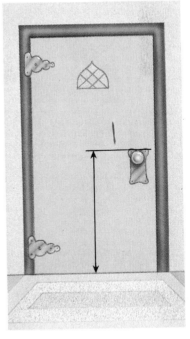

1 meter
(1 m)

A centimeter is a small unit. To measure the length or height of big things, you can use a larger standard unit called a **meter**. The pictures show the length or height of some things measured in meters.

You have learned that the amount of space matter takes up is called volume. Look at the first picture. Which container has the greatest volume of liquid?

You can measure the volume of liquids with units called **liters**. You can use a measuring cup to measure in liters. The girl in the picture has a one-liter measuring cup. One liter will fill four large glasses.

1 liter
(1 L)

Sometimes you want to know which
of two things is heavier. You can use a
balance to compare the masses of two
things. Look at the picture. The balance
shows that the marbles have more mass
than the feathers have.

1 gram
(1 g)

There are standard units for measuring mass. You can use **grams** to measure the mass of small things. The pieces of metal you see in the pictures are called standard masses. They are used to measure in grams.

Look at the picture of the marbles. The standard masses add up to 989 grams. What is the mass of all the marbles?

Look at the picture of the feathers. The standard masses add up to 7 grams. What is the mass of all the feathers?

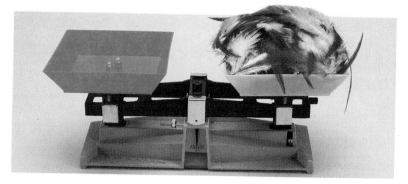

25 kilograms

30 kilograms

1 kilogram
(1 kg)

750 kilograms

The mass of heavier things is measured in units called **kilograms**. Do you know your mass in kilograms? Try to find out. Some scales measure mass in kilograms.

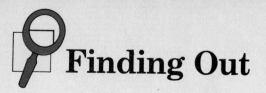

Finding Out

Use these things:
1-L measuring cup
water
short, fat container
tall, thin container

Find out more about volume.

1. Put water into the measuring cup. Stop when the top of the water is at the 1-liter mark.

2. Pour the water into a short, fat container that has a 1-liter mark on it. Find out if the shape changes. Find out if the volume changes.

3. Pour the water back into the first container. Find out what changes.

4. Use a tall, thin container that has a 1-liter mark on it. Do steps 2 and 3 again.

Did the water change shape?

Did the water change volume?

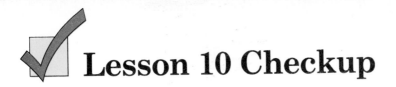

Lesson 10 Checkup

1. Which unit would you use to measure each thing?

centimeter
meter

gram
kilogram

centimeter
meter

2. Which one has more mass?

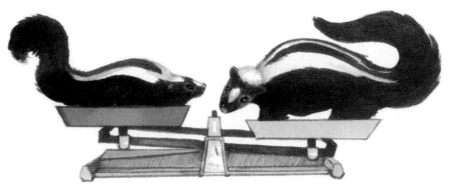

3. Think! Name the different ways that you could measure the box and the juice. What unit would you use for each measurement?

Lesson 11
Magnets

Getting Started

Using a Magnet

1. Get a magnet.

2. Try to pull things with the magnet.

3. Make a chart. Show things a magnet will pull. Show things a magnet will not pull.

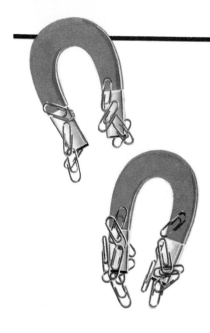

A magnet is an object that pulls some things to it. Magnets come in many shapes and sizes. Some magnets are stronger than others.

All magnets are alike in one way. They pull the same kinds of things. Most things they pull are metal. But a magnet will not pull all metal things.

You know a magnet can pull a nail. This can happen even if something is between the magnet and the nail. In the pictures, what is between each magnet and nail?

Look at the pictures below. The magnet is not pulling the car in the second picture. Why not?

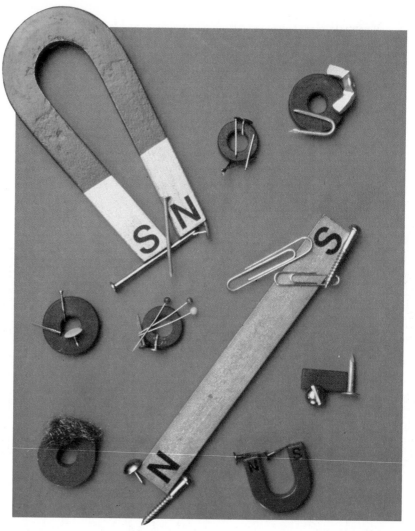

The pull of a magnet is strongest at the **poles**. Each magnet has two poles. There is a north pole and a south pole. Where are the poles on the magnets in the top picture?

Poles that are different will pull each other. A north pole and a south pole will pull each other.

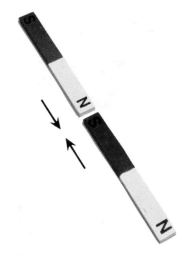

Poles that are alike will push each other away. Two north poles will push each other away.

What will happen in the picture when the magnets get close to each other? What will happen when two south poles are close together?

Magnets can be very useful. The pictures show some ways that magnets are used. How do you use magnets?

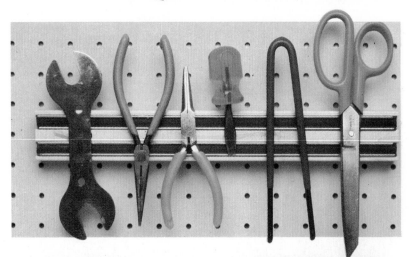

Magnets are also used in many places where you cannot see them. Magnets are needed to make motors work. There are magnets in televisions, telephones, and computers.

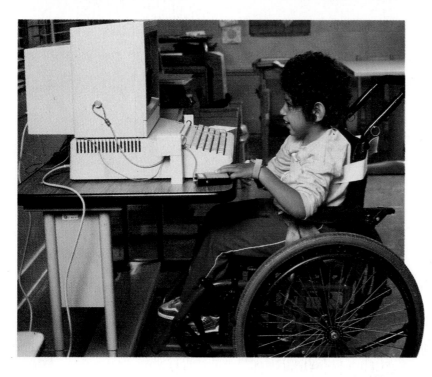

 **Finding Out**

Use these things:
    nail
    magnet

Find out how to make a magnet.

1. Rub the nail with the magnet. Rub it about 30 times. Rub the same way each time.

2. The nail should now be a magnet. Test it to find out.

Does the nail pull the things that a magnet pulls?

✓ Lesson 11 Checkup

1. Which things will a magnet pull?

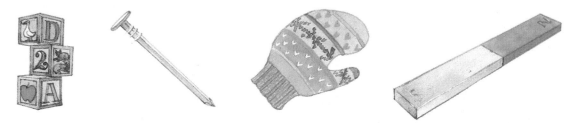

2. Where are the poles of these magnets?

3. Think! What keeps the top magnet from falling down?

Lesson 12
Light

Getting Started

Using Light to See

1. Use a box with a lid, a picture, tape, and a pencil.

2. ◊ **Sharp!** Tape the picture in the box. Make a hole in the other end of the box.

3. Put the lid on the box. Look through the hole. Can you see the picture?

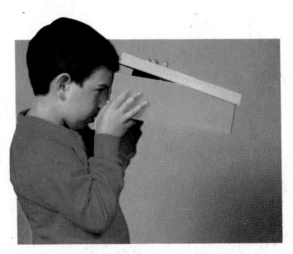

4. Lift the lid just a little. Now can you see the picture? Take the lid off. What can you see now?

We need light to see things. If there is no light, we cannot see anything.

Most of the light on earth comes from the sun. The sun is a **source** of light. A source of light is anything that gives off light energy.

Light is used in many ways. Plants need light to live and grow. Plants use light energy from the sun to make food.

Animals use light, too. The bobcat in the bottom picture is using light to find food.

We do not always have light from the sun. Sometimes we use light from other sources. A light bulb is a light source. Fire is a light source, too.

Some sources give off a lot of light energy. They make a **bright** light. Other sources make only a **dim** light.

People have many uses for light. We use light for working and playing. We use light for safety. How is light being used in each picture?

What would your life be like if you did not have many sources of light?

Most things we see are not light sources. They **reflect** light. Light from a light source bounces off them.

The picture shows how this works. The flashlight is the light source. The mirror reflects the light.

Most objects reflect light in many directions. We see an object if some of the reflected light travels to our eyes.

In bright light, we can see many colors.
In dim light, it is hard to see dark colors.

Yellow and orange are easy to see in
bright light and in dim light. We use these
colors for safety.

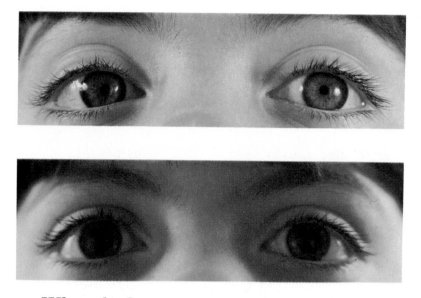

When light enters our eyes, we can see. Light goes into a small hole in the center of the eye. This hole is called the **pupil**. The pupil looks like a small black circle.

The size of the pupil can change. In bright light, the pupil gets smaller. It lets in less light. When the light is dim, the pupil gets larger. It lets in more light.

Many animals have pupils that can change size, too.

It is important to take care of your eyes. A doctor can check your eyes.

Never look straight into the sun or other very bright light sources. You could hurt your eyes.

The people in the pictures are keeping their eyes safe.

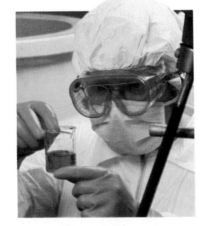

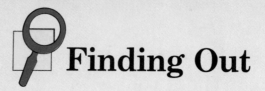 **Finding Out**

Use these things:
scissors
box with lid
2 mirrors
tape

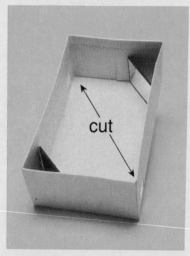

cut

Find out how mirrors reflect light.

1. ◇ **Sharp!** Cut two holes in the box. The first picture shows where to cut.

2. Tape the mirrors in the box. The first picture shows where to put them.

3. Put the lid on the box.

4. Look through the bottom hole.

Can you see something that is near the top hole? Why or why not?

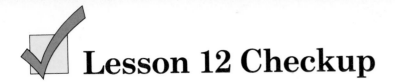

Lesson 12 Checkup

1. Which things are light sources?

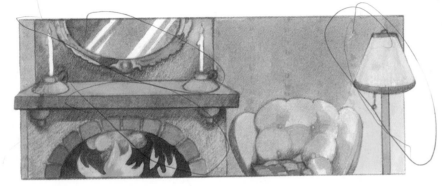

2. Which color is safest in dim light? *one*

3. Think! Jan can see Bill in the mirror.
Can Bill see Jan? *yes*

Lesson 13
Shadow

Getting Started

Finding Out What Stops Light

1. Use plastic wrap, wax paper, and drawing paper. Stand near a sunny window.

2. Hold each piece of paper in front of you. Which stops all the light? Which stops some of the light? Which lets light through?

3. Use some other objects. Guess how much light each object will stop. Then find out.

Light goes through some things. Other things stop light. When light is stopped, you can see a shadow.

In the picture, light is moving from a light source to the wall. It is moving in straight lines. A girl is stopping some of the light. She is making shadow pictures with her hands.

You can make shadow pictures, too. What could you use for a light source?

Some things let a lot of light go through them. They make a pale shadow. Some things stop all the light. When a lot of light is stopped, the shadow is darker.

Shadows can change. Sometimes a shadow gets bigger or smaller. Sometimes it moves to a different place.

Look at the pictures. The shadow has changed. What made the shadow change?

Look at the pictures of the dancer and her shadow. The light is coming from the same place in both pictures, but the shadow of the dancer has moved. What made the shadow change?

 **Finding Out**

Use these things:
tall block
colored chalk

Find out how shadows change during the day.

1. Start in the morning. Set a block on the ground. Trace around the block with chalk. Then trace around its shadow.

2. At noon, trace the shadow again. Use a different color.

3. Trace the shadow again during the afternoon. Use another color.

What happened to the shadow?

Why did it happen?

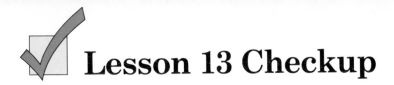

Lesson 13 Checkup

1. Which picture shows how light travels?

A

B

2. Which building made each shadow?

3. Think! How was the picture made?

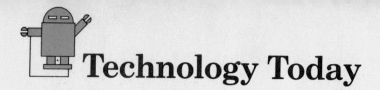

Technology Today

A Super Light

Have you ever seen a **laser** show? A laser is a special light. It is very different from other kinds of light. In a laser show, this light is used to make pictures.

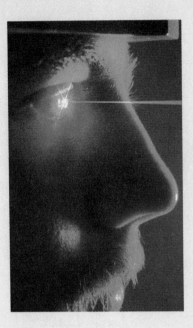

Think of a light bulb. Its light spreads out in all directions. But a laser makes a thin beam of light. The light does not spread out. The beam is strong and straight and steady. It can travel a long, long way.

Lasers have many important uses. They can cut through steel. They can measure distances. They can help doctors. And new uses are being found all the time.

Think About It
If you had a laser, what could you measure with it?

Are there shadows in space?

Ms. Ogden's class
Hatfield Elementary School
Hatfield,
Pennsylvania

Dr. Basri is an **astronomer**. He studies the stars. He uses telescopes to look into space.

Dr. Basri says shadows form in space in the same way as they do on earth. Three things are needed. First, a light source is needed. Second, there must be something to stop some of the light. Third, there must be an object on which the shadow can be seen.

Look at the picture of the spaceship. The sun is the light source. The astronaut is stopping some of the light. He is between the sun and the door of the spaceship, so you can see his shadow on the door. You can find some other shadows in this picture, too.

Gibor Basri

Dr. Basri says there are not as many shadows in space as on earth. This is because there are not very many objects in space. And the objects are often too far apart for the shadow of one to be seen on another.

Unit Three
Earth Science

Earth science is about the land and water that make up the earth. But earth science is about much more than the earth itself. It is also about the air above the earth. And it is about the sun, moon, and stars.

In this unit, you will learn about the earth's water and weather. You will learn about the moon. And you will learn about day and night.

Lesson 14
Water

Getting Started

Learning About the Earth's Water

1. Get a map of the world, some blocks or other small objects, and some graph paper.

2. The blue parts of the map are water. Cover the blue parts with blocks. Then count the blocks as you take them away.

3. The other parts of the map are land. Find out how many blocks will cover these parts.

4. Make a bar graph. Make one bar for water and another bar for land. Color one square for each block.

Water is all around us. There are huge oceans. There are wide rivers and narrow streams. There are ponds and lakes. In the coldest parts of the world, there is ice. There is a lot more water than land on earth.

pond

river

lake

iceberg

Water falls to the ground as rain. Some of the rain runs off the ground into streams. When streams come together, they form rivers. The rivers flow toward the oceans.

salt water

fresh water

Most of the earth's water is in the oceans. Ocean water is called **salt water**. You cannot see the salt, but you can taste it.

The water in most lakes and rivers is not salty. It is called **fresh water**.

All living things need water. Some plants and animals need salt water. Others need fresh water. People need to drink lots of clean, fresh water every day. We cannot drink salt water.

Look at the pictures. Which living things need salt water? Which living things need fresh water?

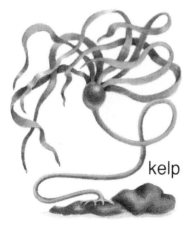

kelp

A lot of our food comes from the ocean. We call this food "seafood." Lobsters, shrimp, oysters, and clams are seafoods. Fish is our most important seafood. We also eat many fish from fresh water.

There are water plants that people eat, too. One of them is a seaweed called **kelp**. Have you ever eaten it? You may have eaten kelp without knowing it. Kelp is sometimes used in making ice cream.

People use water in many other ways. We use water for cooking and cleaning. We use water in our factories. We swim in water and skate on ice. We put out fires with water. We travel on water in ships and boats. Can you think of other ways we use water?

Sometimes water becomes **polluted**. Polluted water is not safe. It has harmful wastes in it. The wastes come from farms and cities. Polluted water often looks dirty. But sometimes we cannot see the pollution.

Polluted water can kill plants and animals that live in the water. It can make people sick. It is important to keep our water clean.

Do you know where the water in your home comes from? In some places, water for homes comes from underground wells. In other places, it comes from lakes or rivers. Most well water is quite clean. The water from lakes and rivers is usually cleaned before people drink it. The large picture shows water being cleaned in a water treatment plant.

Finding Out

Use these things:
2 clear plastic cups
labels
salt water
fresh water
2 stirrers
hand lens

Compare salt water and fresh water.

1. Label one cup "salt water." Put a little salt water into that cup. Label the other cup "fresh water," and put fresh water into it.

2. Compare the color and smell of the fresh water and salt water.

3. ◇ **Be careful!** Use the stirrers to compare taste. Taste just a drop from each cup.

4. Put the cups in a warm place. Wait until all the water is gone.

5. Use a hand lens. Look inside both cups.

How are salt water and fresh water alike?

How are they different?

✓ Lesson 14 Checkup

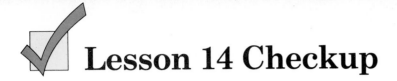

1. You can skate on me. When I melt, I am water. What am I?

2. Boats float on me. My water is salty. What am I?

3. Most of my surface is water. The rest is land. What am I?

4. You may not be able to see me, but I can make you sick. I can make water unsafe to drink. What am I?

5. **Think!** Imagine there was no water in your town for a day. What would happen?

Lesson 15
The Moving Earth

Getting Started

Finding the Sun in the Sky

1. Use drawing paper, crayons, clock pictures, scissors, and glue.

2. Draw three pictures of the same place. Draw them in the morning, at noon, and in the afternoon.

3. Each time, find the sun in the sky. Put the sun in your picture. Do not stare at the sun.

4. Glue a clock onto each picture. Show the time that you drew each one.

Some things change. Some things stay the same. Other things change in the same way over and over again.

Every morning the sun **rises** in the east. The sky becomes light and day begins. Every evening the sun **sets** in the west. The sky becomes dark and night begins.

The sun rises and sets every day. It changes in the same way every day.

Some things seem to move when they really are not moving. Have you been on a merry-go-round? Things around the merry-go-round seem to be moving. But they are not moving. You are moving.

The sun seems to move, too. It seems to move across the sky. But it is not really moving across the sky. The earth is moving. This makes the sun seem to move.

The earth moves in two ways. It spins like a top. It also moves in a circle around the sun.

Look at the picture of the girl and the lamp. Pretend that the girl is the earth. Pretend that the lamp is the sun. The girl is moving in two ways at the same time. She is spinning. And she is moving around the lamp. She is moving in the same two ways that the earth moves.

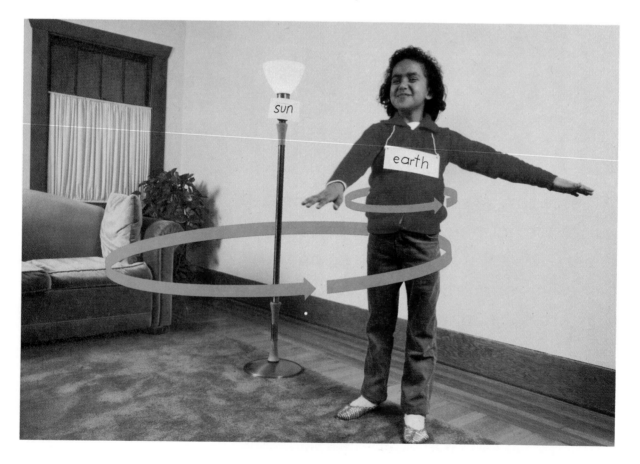

The earth spins around once each day. You cannot feel or see the earth spin. Yet the earth is always spinning.

one day

The earth circles the sun once each year. You cannot feel or see the earth circling the sun. Yet the earth is always circling.

one year

Look at the picture of the light shining on the ball. Only half of the ball gets light. Now look at the picture of the earth. The earth is shaped like a ball. Only half of the earth gets light at one time.

The sun is always shining on the earth. The earth is always spinning. Parts of the earth turn into and out of the light. It takes one day to make one complete turn.

The part of the earth that is facing the sun has day. The part that is facing away from the sun has night.

The sun keeps shining. The earth keeps turning. Day changes to night. Night changes to day. This happens over and over again.

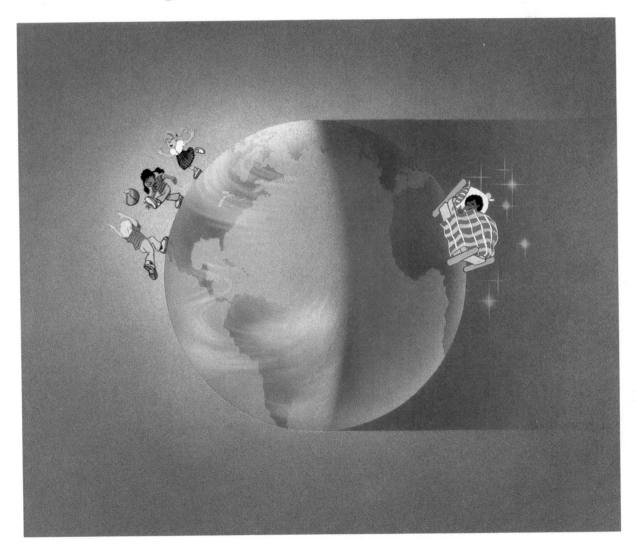

 **Finding Out**

Use these things:
paper house
tape
globe
flashlight

Find out how the sun lights the earth.

1. Find where you live on the globe. Tape a paper house to the globe at that place.

2. Make the room very dark.

3. Shine the light on the globe. Half of the globe should be lighted. Half should be in the dark. Make sure your house is in the light.

4. Turn the globe until your house is not in the light. Keep turning it until your house is lighted again.

How much of the earth has day at one time?

Why does day change to night?

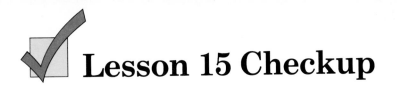

Lesson 15 Checkup

1. Tell how day is different from night.

2. Which picture shows a day? Which one shows a year?

3. Think! Draw a picture of the earth. Next, draw the sun. Color the day side of the earth yellow. Color the night side black.

Lesson 16
The Moon

Getting Started

Making a Moon Calendar

1. Use a calendar, some paper circles, a pencil, scissors, and glue.

2. Look for the moon. Draw its shape on a circle. Cut out the shape.

3. Find the date on the calendar. Glue the shape on that square.

4. Do this every night or morning for one month.

The moon is our nearest neighbor in space. It is smaller than the earth. The moon has no water or air. It is covered with rocks and dust. Nothing lives on the moon.

The moon has tall mountains. It also has large flat places called **plains**. There are many holes called **craters** on the plains. Some craters are small, but others are very big.

Astronauts are people who go into space in spaceships. Some astronauts have gone to the moon. The astronauts walked on the moon. They brought rocks and dust from the moon back to the earth. The astronauts helped people to learn more about the moon.

The moon does not make its own light. The sun shines on the moon. The moon reflects light from the sun. We see the reflected light.

The sun always lights up half the moon. But we do not always see all of the lighted half. This is because the moon moves around the earth. It travels around the earth once each month. When the moon is in different places, we see different amounts of light.

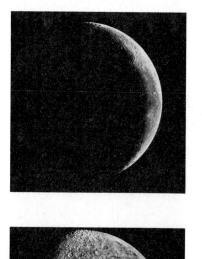

8:00 p.m.

10:00 p.m.

1:00 a.m.

We see the moon move across the sky. Like the sun, it seems to rise in the east and set in the west. Although the moon moves, it does not move in this way. It seems to rise and set each day because the earth is spinning.

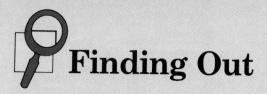 # Finding Out

Use these things:
pictures of the moon
clay
rocks

Make a model of the moon's land.

1. Look at pictures of the moon. Find plains, mountains, and craters.

2. Make one of the moon's plains out of clay.

3. Add a mountain.

4. Use rocks to make craters in the plain. Make some big craters and some little ones.

How is the land on the moon like the land on the earth?

How is it different?

✓ Lesson 16 Checkup

1. The moon travels around the ____?____.

2. The moon's light comes from the ____?____.

3. The earth's nearest neighbor is the ____?____.

4. **Think!** Which things are not on the moon?

Lesson 17
Air and Weather

Getting Started

Measuring Air Temperature

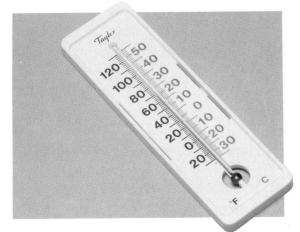

1. Use a thermometer.

2. Find a place outdoors to put the thermometer.

3. Look at the thermometer in the morning. Write down the time and temperature.

4. Do this again before lunch and in the afternoon. Find out if the temperature changes.

Air is all around the earth. We cannot see air. We cannot taste it or smell it. But we can feel it.

The air is always changing. It may feel cold or warm. It may move fast or slow. It may be wet or dry.

Changes in the air cause our **weather**. The weather changes from day to day and from season to season.

1:00 p.m.

7:00 p.m.

The earth and the air are warmed by the sun. It is usually warmer in the day and cooler at night. In many places, it is hot in summer and cold in winter. We can feel the air temperature change.

Heat makes the air move. Moving air is called **wind**. The wind can blow from any direction. It can blow fast or slow. Sometimes the air does not move.

How fast is the wind blowing in each picture?

When the wind blows, it can move many things. It can move the clouds. It can move leaves and sand. What other things can the wind move?

People need to know how the weather will change. Farmers want to know if it will be warm enough for seeds to grow. Sailors want to know if it will be windy. Everyone needs to plan what to wear.

Scientists predict the weather. They tell how the weather might change. But it is not always possible to know. The weather often surprises us.

Cars, trucks, and factories can put unhealthy things into the air. We call this **air pollution**. You can see air pollution in the top picture. The air looks dirty.

Sometimes we cannot see air pollution. In the bottom picture, the air looks clean. But there may be some pollution in it. Sometimes winds blow pollution to farms and forests.

Pollution can harm plants and animals. People must learn how to keep the air clean.

 **Finding Out**

Use these things:
crepe paper
ruler
tape

Find out how the wind is blowing.

1. Tape pieces of crepe paper to a ruler.

2. Go outside. Watch the way the paper moves. Is the wind moving fast or slow? Where is it blowing from?

3. Go to another place. You might stand near a building. Watch the paper again.

How is the wind different in the two places?

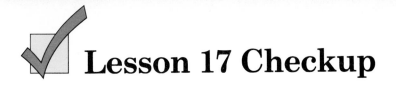

Lesson 17 Checkup

1. Sometimes when you go out to play,
I try to blow your hat away.
What am I?

2. You will find me in the air.
Cars and factories put me there.
If I travel to a farm,
I may do a lot of harm.
What am I?

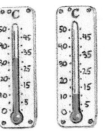

3. In the summer, I am hot.
In the winter, I am not.
I have no color, taste, or smell.
Even so, you know me well.
What am I?

4. Think! Where is the wind coming from?
Which way are the clouds moving?

Lesson 18
Clouds and Storms

Getting Started

Making Cloud Pictures

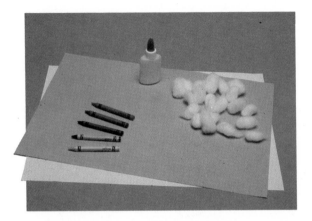

1. Use drawing paper, crayons, cotton balls, and glue.

2. Go outside or look out a window. Look at the clouds.

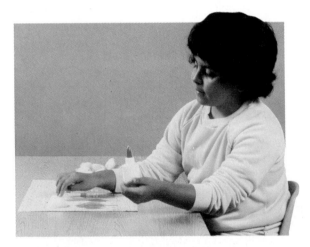

3. Draw a picture. Draw the clouds you saw. Glue cotton onto the clouds.

4. Look at clouds on other days. Draw a picture with a different kind of cloud.

Clouds form from water vapor in the air. They form when the air gets cool. There are many kinds of clouds.

Fog is one kind of cloud. It forms near the ground.

Other clouds form high above the ground. Some are white and fluffy. Some look like thin feathers. Both kinds of clouds usually mean fair weather.

Other clouds are thick and dark. They often cover the sky. Thick dark clouds can bring rainstorms or snowstorms.

There are many kinds of storms. **Thunderstorms** bring lots of rain. They have lightning and thunder. Thunderstorms also have strong winds.

Blizzards bring lots of snow and cold. Winds blow very hard during a blizzard. They blow the snow around.

tornado

hurricane

Hurricanes are very large storms. Winds blow very fast. There is a lot of rain. Hurricanes begin over the ocean. They often move toward land.

Tornadoes also have very fast winds. The winds spin like a top. The winds form a cloud that may touch the ground. Tornadoes can destroy everything in their path.

Storms can harm buildings. They can harm trees and other plants. Storms can also be dangerous to people. Here are some storm safety tips:

- Stay indoors during a storm.
- Do not stand under trees when there is lightning.
- Stay out of water when there is lightning.
- Stay away from windows when the wind is blowing hard.
- Keep a flashlight and other things you might need in a safe place. What else might you need?

Finding Out

Use these things:
plastic bottle
bottle lid
water
1 spoonful of salt
dropper
dishwashing liquid

Find out how a tornado moves.

1. Put water into the bottle. Leave about three centimeters of space at the top.

2. Add the salt. Put the lid on the bottle and shake it.

3. Add a drop of dishwashing liquid. Make sure that you add only one small drop.

4. ◇ **Be careful!** Put the lid on the bottle again. Move the bottle around in a circle.

Did you see a tornado?

Lesson 18 Checkup

1. How are these clouds different?

2. Which of these clouds will bring rain?
Why?

3. Think! What is wrong in each picture?

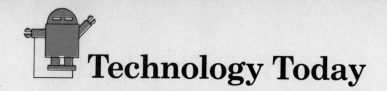

Technology Today

Weather Pictures from Space

No one can know for sure what the weather will be. But scientists try to make good predictions. To do this, they need special tools.

One tool is the **weather satellite**. Satellites are put into space by rockets. They move in a circle far above the earth.

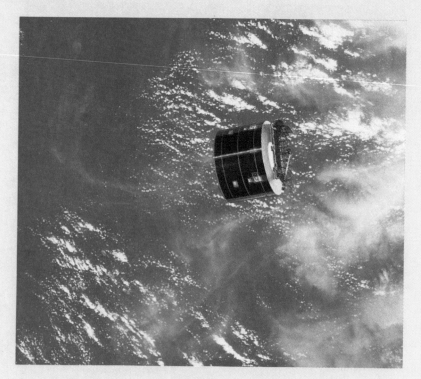

Every day, the satellites take pictures of the earth. The pictures are sent to weather stations. From the pictures, scientists can see where clouds are forming. They can tell how the clouds are moving. They can predict changes in the weather all over the earth.

Think About It

How could a weather satellite help to warn people of a bad storm?

How do weather satellites make it easier to plan for the weekend?

Ask a Scientist

Will there always be enough good land to grow our food on?

Ms. Teepen's class
Ira J. Earl School Las Vegas, Nevada

Mr. Holl is a scientist who studies how to grow plants. He is called a **horticulturist**. He has worked with tomatoes, corn, and other plants that we eat. Mr. Holl says that people are working together to make sure there will always be enough good farmland.

First, we are learning better ways to take care of the farmland we have. We are finding ways of keeping wind and water from carrying away good soil.

We are making new kinds of weed
and bug killers that do not hurt the soil.
And we are changing ways of growing
food so that we get more food from the
same amount of land.

We are also looking for ways to bring
water to land that is now too dry to farm.
This could give us even more good land
to grow food on.

In years to come, we may find that
more of our food comes from the ocean.
People are learning to farm the ocean as
they now farm the land.

Lawrence Holl

Health Science

Health science is about the parts of your body and how they work. It is also about how to take care of your body.

In this unit, you will learn about the inside of your body. You will learn what you can do to be healthy. And you will learn how other people can help you to be healthy.

Lesson 19
Parts of Your Body

Getting Started

Naming Body Parts

1. Use crayons, small paper strips, large paper, paints, paintbrushes, and tape.

2. Your teacher will write the names of some body parts on the chalkboard. Copy them onto the paper strips.

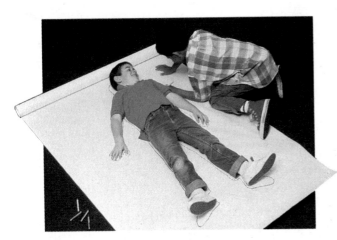 

3. Lie down on the large paper. Have someone draw around your body.

4. Paint your picture. Then tape the names of the body parts onto the picture.

209

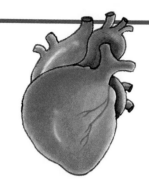

The human body has many parts. Some parts are on the outside of the body. They are easy to see. Other body parts cannot be seen. They are inside the body.

Some body parts are called **organs**. An organ does a special job for the body. You can see the organs of the senses. But most organs are inside the body.

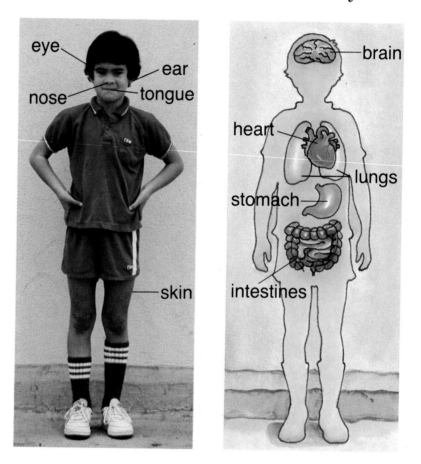

eye · ear · nose · tongue · skin

brain · heart · lungs · stomach · intestines

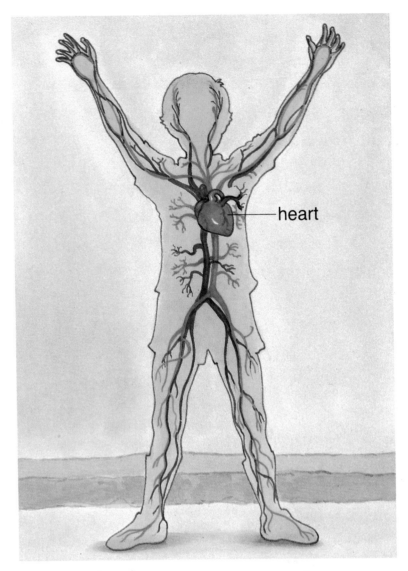

heart

Your **heart** is an organ inside your chest. It is about as big as your fist. The heart is made of muscle. It works harder than any other muscle in your body. Your heart beats all the time. Each time it beats, it pumps blood through your body.

Your **lungs** are also inside your chest. You have two lungs. When you breathe, air goes in and out of your lungs. Air has a gas called **oxygen** in it. You must have oxygen to live.

Watch your chest move when you breathe. Take a deep breath. Then let it go. When does your chest get bigger? When does it get smaller?

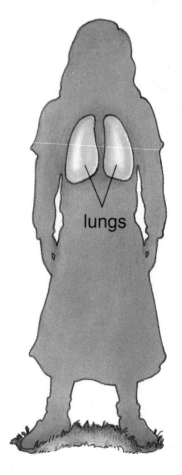

lungs

Your heart and lungs work together. The heart pumps blood into the lungs. When the blood is in the lungs, it gets oxygen. Then the blood takes the oxygen to other parts of your body.

Exercise is good for your heart and lungs. It helps your heart work better. It helps your lungs take in more air.

Your **stomach** is an organ that changes food. Food must be changed before your body can use it. Liquid is added, and the food is broken into tiny pieces.

When food leaves your stomach, it goes to organs called the **intestines**. The food is changed some more. Some of this food moves into your blood. The blood carries it throughout your body.

Your body cannot use all parts of the food. The parts that cannot be used leave your body.

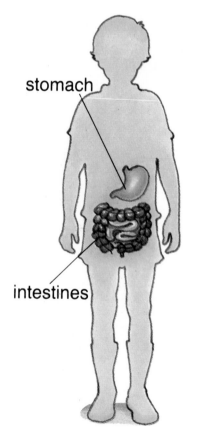

stomach

intestines

Your **brain** is an important organ. If you did not have a brain, you could not think. Your brain gets information from your eyes, nose, tongue, ears, and skin. Then it helps your body act. It tells your muscles what to do.

You use your brain to think about things that you want to do. When you want to climb, you think about it first. Then your brain tells your muscles how to move.

There are some things your brain controls that you do not have to think about. You do not have to think about breathing or yawning. You do not have to think about making your heart beat.

All the parts of your body work together. Blood carries food and oxygen throughout your body. Your heart keeps the blood moving. Your lungs put oxygen into the blood. Your stomach and intestines help change food so other parts of your body can use it. Your brain helps keep all parts of your body working together. The parts work together to keep your body alive and healthy.

 **Finding Out**

Use these things:
paper bag
scissors
markers

Draw organs of the body.

1. Cut a hole in the bottom of the bag. Make the hole big enough to fit over your head. Then cut holes for your arms.

2. Draw the heart, lungs, and stomach on the bag.

3. Put the bag on.

Are the organs in the right places?

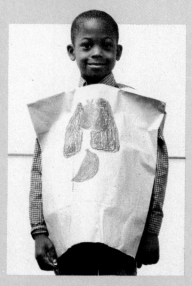

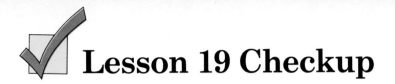

Lesson 19 Checkup

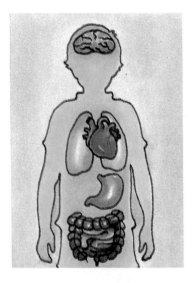

1. Your ___?___ take in oxygen.

2. Your ___?___ pumps blood.

3. Your ___?___ and ___?___ help change food so your body can use it.

4. Your ___?___ controls what you think and do.

5. **Think!** Feel the part of your body where your brain is. Then feel where your heart, lungs, and stomach are. What keeps these organs safe?

Lesson 20
Good Health

Getting Started

Recording How You Spend Your Time

1. Use some paper and a clock or watch. Fold the paper into three parts.

2. Write these words at the top of your paper: "exercise," "quiet time," and "sleep."

3. Look at a clock when you begin to do something. When you stop, look at the clock again. Write down how much time you spent.

4. Add up how many hours you spent doing each kind of thing. Do this for two days.

We each have our own body to take care of. Keeping your body healthy is a big job. You can make choices that will be good for your health. For example, you can get exercise every day.

Exercise makes your muscles stronger. Stronger muscles help you work and play longer. People exercise in many ways. How do you exercise?

You can also make sure that you get enough rest. You need to rest after working or playing. You need to sleep many hours each night. Sleep helps you stay well. It also helps you grow. Children need more sleep than adults do because children are growing.

Look at the pictures below. They show more healthy choices. What other things can you do to stay healthy?

Being clean helps you to be healthy. Wash your hands well before you eat and after going to the bathroom. Keep your body and hair clean. Clean your teeth by brushing them after you eat.

Staying clean helps to keep some **germs** away. Germs are tiny living things. They are too small to see, but they are all around you. Some germs can make you sick if they get into your body.

Wearing the right clothes can also keep you healthy. Clothes can help your body to stay at the right temperature. The pictures show children wearing clothes for different weather. How do you know which clothes to wear each day?

Food helps your body stay strong and healthy. For example, milk and cheese help make your teeth and bones strong. Some fruits help your eyes and skin. Other foods help other parts of your body.

Scientists have put foods into four groups. You should eat foods from each group every day. Each group helps your body in different ways. The pictures on these two pages show you the four food groups.

milk group

bread and cereal group

Some foods do not help your body as much as other foods. Most cakes, cookies, and candy do not help much. Some people eat too many of these foods. They feel full, but their bodies do not get all the things they need.

Your body also needs lots of water every day. Water is in everything you drink. You also get some of the water you need from foods. Water is in foods such as soup, fruits, and vegetables. But you need to drink plain water, too.

vegetable and fruit group

meat and bean group

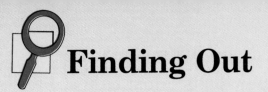 **Finding Out**

Use these things:
crayons
paper dishes
drawing paper
knife, fork, spoon
paper napkin
tape or glue

Plan a meal for your family.

1. Pick breakfast, lunch, or dinner. Choose foods for your family to eat.

2. Draw the foods on the paper dishes.

3. Draw a placemat on the drawing paper. Glue or tape the other things to it.

4. Write the name of the meal.

Did you choose foods from all four food groups?

Did you plan a healthy meal?

Lesson 20 Checkup

1. What are two ways that sleep helps you?

2. Why is it important to stay clean?

3. Think! Which food does not belong in each group?

Lesson 21
Health Care

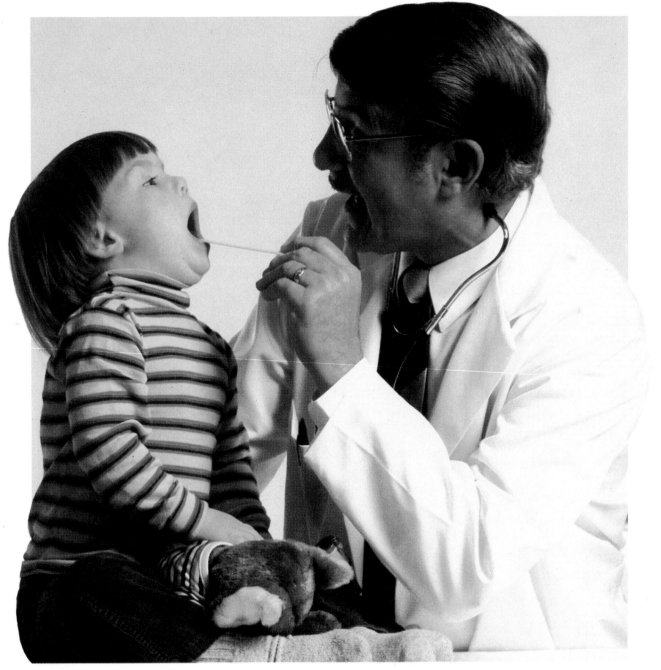

Getting Started

Listening to Your Heart

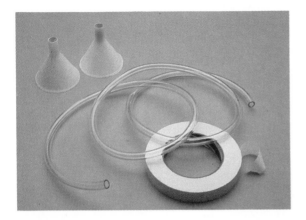

1. Get two funnels, a rubber tube, and some tape.

2. Tape one funnel to each end of the tube.

3. Put one funnel next to your ear. Put the other funnel over your heart. Listen to your heartbeat.

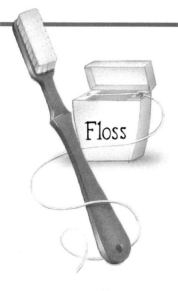

Floss

You can take care of your health in many ways. Health-care workers also can help you stay healthy.

You should go to the dentist for a **dental checkup** twice a year. Dentists check your teeth and gums. They clean your teeth. They can also show you how to take good care of your teeth.

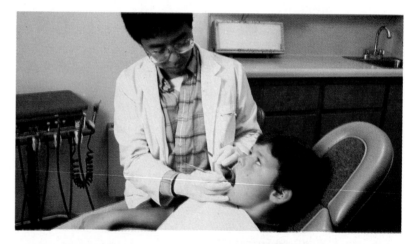

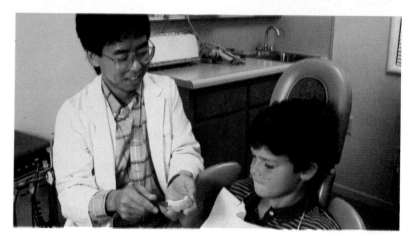

You should also have a **medical checkup** each year. A doctor and nurse will check many parts of your body. A checkup may find health problems that are just beginning. Then health-care workers can help you.

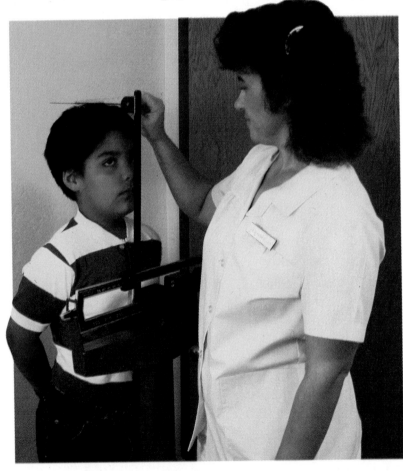

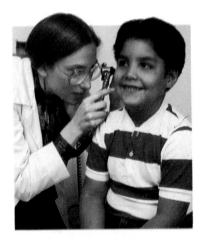

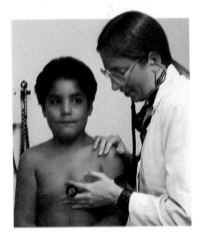

Look at the pictures. What things are being checked? What are some other things that are checked during a medical checkup?

Doctors and nurses also give you **vaccines**. Vaccines will keep you from getting some kinds of sicknesses. Some vaccines are given in shots. Others can be swallowed.

Most people do not like to get shots. But getting a shot is better than getting sick.

Most people get sick sometimes, even if they take good care of themselves. Sickness is often caused by germs. Germs are everywhere. You cannot always keep harmful germs out of your body.

Germs can sometimes travel from one person to another. If you have a cold, be careful around other people. Cover your mouth when you cough or sneeze. Wash your hands before you touch things other people will use.

Sometimes you go to the doctor because you are sick. You might get some medicine to help you get well. Adults in your family can help you take your medicine. They make sure you take it at the right time. They give you the right amount.

You should never take medicine by yourself. Medicine can be dangerous if it is not taken in the right way.

Sometimes when you are sick you do not need a doctor. You may not need to take any medicine. Good food and extra rest are all you need to get well.

Finding Out

Use these things:
drawing paper
markers

Make a get-well card.

1. Make a card. Draw something cheerful on the front of it.

2. Inside, write a good wish. You could write "I hope you will get well soon."

3. Save the card until someone you know is sick. Then send that person the card.

If you were sick, what might help make you feel better?

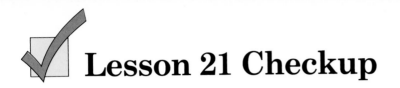

Lesson 21 Checkup

1. Which is better to do when you are healthy? Which is better to do when you are sick?

2. _____?_____ will keep you from getting some kinds of sicknesses.

Germs   Vaccines   Sneezes

3. **Think!** Why do most medicine bottles have safety caps?

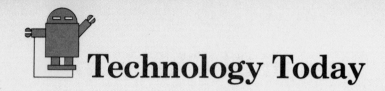

Technology Today

Looking Inside the Body

Doctors can see the inside of the body with special pictures. Doctors use what they learn from these pictures to help people get well.

An **X ray** is one kind of picture of the inside of the body. You may have had X rays taken of your teeth. In an X ray, hard things such as teeth and bones look white. A doctor can see if a bone is broken. A dentist can see if a tooth is unhealthy.

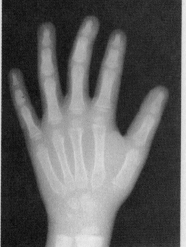

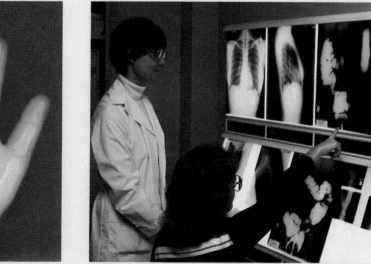

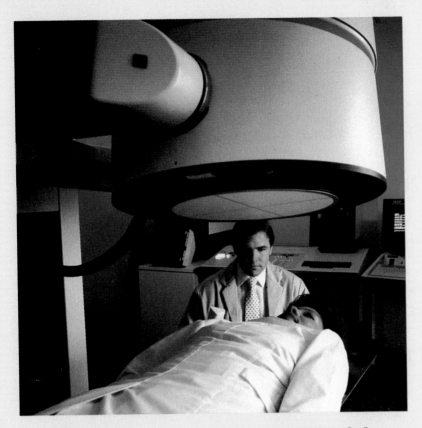

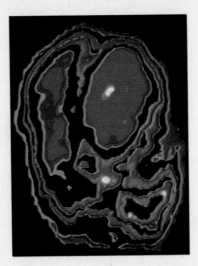

A **body scan** is also a picture of the inside of the body. The doctor sees the pictures on a computer screen. Body scans can show problems with the organs inside the body. The scan in the picture at the right shows a person's heart.

Think About It

What would happen if doctors did not have X rays and body scans to see inside our bodies?

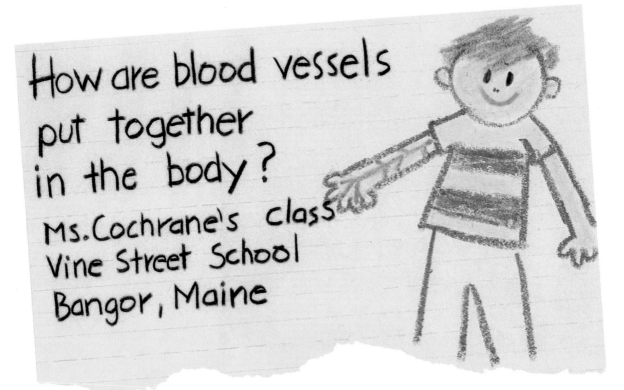

How are blood vessels
put together
in the body?

Ms. Cochrane's class
Vine Street School
Bangor, Maine

Dr. Jungery studies diseases of the blood. She is a **biologist**, a scientist who works with living things.

Dr. Jungery says that blood vessels are put together something like a group of streets and highways. Blood leaves the heart in large blood vessels that are like super highways. These "super highways" turn into smaller "highways," then into "streets."

242

Finally, the blood moves through the smallest blood vessels. The smallest blood vessels reach every part of the body. The blood brings food and oxygen to every part of the body. It also picks up wastes.

Then the blood begins its trip back to the heart. It goes from the smallest blood vessels to larger ones. It travels on different "streets" and "highways" to get back to the heart. Then it begins a new trip.

Michele Jungery

Glossary

A

air pollution page 191
Unhealthy things in the air.
*Dirty smoke coming from
factories makes air pollution.*

astronaut page 179
A person who travels in space.
*Astronauts have gone to the
moon.*

astronomer page 150
A scientist who studies stars,
planets, and other things in
space. *We asked an astronomer
to tell us about the stars.*

B

balance page 113
A tool used to compare the mass
of something to a known mass, or
to find out which of two things is
heavier. *The balance shows that
a nickel is heavier than a dime.*

biologist page 242
A scientist who studies living
things. *A student who likes
animals might want to be a
biologist.*

blizzard page 197
A storm with strong winds and
snow. *The blizzard blew snow up
to our second-floor window.*

body scan page 241
A picture of the inside of the
body. *The doctor looked at the
body scan on the computer screen.*

brain page 215
The organ of the body that
controls everything that you do.
*Your brain tells your heart when
to beat.*

bright page 132
Giving a large amount of light. *The new light bulb gave off a bright light.*

C

centimeter (cm) page 110
A standard unit used to measure height or length. *My crayon is nine centimeters long.*

cone page 69
The part of some plants where seeds are found. *We made dolls from the cones of pine trees.*

crater page 178
A hole in the ground that is shaped like a bowl. *If you use a telescope, you can see craters on the moon.*

D

dental checkup page 232
A visit to the dentist to see if your teeth and gums are healthy. *We have a dental checkup twice a year.*

dim page 132
Giving off very little light. *The light from the candle was dim.*

E

endangered page 39
In danger of no longer being alive. *The bald eagle is an endangered animal and may become extinct.*

extinct page 31
No longer alive. *Dinosaurs are extinct animals.*

F

fog page 196
A kind of cloud that forms near the ground. *It was hard to see the trees through the fog.*

fossil page 16
A trace of a plant or animal that lived long ago. *Dinosaur bones are fossils.*

freeze page 102
Turn from a liquid into a solid. *I will freeze the water to make ice.*

fresh water page 158
Water that is not salty. *Rivers have fresh water.*

G

gas page 96
A state of matter that has no shape or size of its own. *There are many gases in the air.*

germ page 224
A tiny living thing that cannot be seen. *Keeping clean helps to keep some germs from getting into your body.*

grafting page 82
Joining two plants together to make them grow as if they were one plant. *The farmer was grafting a new branch onto the tree.*

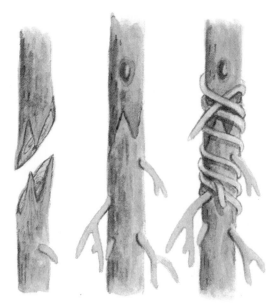

gram (g) page 114
A standard unit used to measure the mass of small things. *The mass of a nickel is about five grams.*

H
heart page 211
The organ that pumps blood through the body. *Your heart is in your chest.*

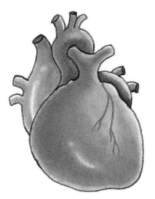

horticulturist page 204
A scientist who studies how to grow plants. *We asked a horticulturist to help us decide what plants to grow on our farm.*

hurricane page 198
A large storm with fast winds and a lot of rain. *Hurricanes start over the ocean.*

I
intestine page 214
An organ that helps change food so the body can use it. *The body has two intestines. They look like long curled-up tubes.*

invisible page 92
Cannot be seen. *Wind is invisible, but we can feel it.*

K
kelp page 160
A water plant that people can eat. *Kelp is a kind of seaweed that is long and brown.*

kilogram (kg) page 115
A standard unit used to measure mass. *My cat has a mass of about four kilograms.*

L

laser page 148
A strong, narrow beam of light that is very useful. *A laser light can cut metal.*

liquid page 95
A state of matter that can change shape but does not change its volume. *Milk is a liquid.*

liter (L) page 112
A standard unit used to measure volume. *This bottle holds two liters of milk.*

lung page 212
One of a pair of organs that help you breathe. *When you breathe in, your lungs fill with air.*

M

mass page 91
The amount of matter that something has. *An elephant has a large mass.*

matter page 90
What things are made of. All things that take up space and have mass are matter. *Balls, bicycles, and balloons are matter.*

medical checkup page 233
A visit to the doctor to see if your body is healthy. *My doctor makes my medical checkup fun and interesting.*

melt page 102
Change from a solid to a liquid. *We watched the butter melt in the hot sun.*

meter (m) page 111
A standard unit used to measure the length or height of things. *My window is one meter from the floor.*

O

organ page 210
A body part that does a special job for your body. *Your heart and lungs are organs.*

oxygen page 212
A gas in the air. *People need oxygen to live.*

P

paleontologist page 84
A scientist who studies fossils. *A paleontologist told our class about dinosaur fossils.*

parent plant page 47
A plant that makes seeds. *Some seeds from a parent plant will grow into new plants.*

petal page 66
A part of a flower that often is brightly colored. *Some rose petals are red.*

plain page 178
Large flat areas of land. *There are plains in the center of the United States.*

pole page 122
A place on a magnet where the pull is strongest. *The poles of my bar magnet are at the ends.*

pollute page 162
Make something dirty or unsafe. *Polluted air and water are harmful to plants and animals.*

pupil page 136
The opening in the eye that looks like a black circle. *Light goes into the eye through the pupil.*

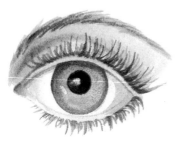

R
reflect page 134
To change the direction of something such as light or sound. *Most objects reflect some light.*

rise page 168
Go up, get higher. *I saw the sun rise early in the morning.*

S
salt water page 158
Water that has salt in it. *Ocean animals need salt water to live.*

seed coat page 48
The tough outside part found on many seeds. *The seed coat keeps the new plant safe.*

seed plant page 46
A plant that grows from a seed. *Plants that have flowers are seed plants.*

seedling page 50
A very young seed plant. *The bean seedling grew from a bean seed.*

set page 168
Go down, get lower. *My father told me to be home before the sun sets.*

solid page 94
Matter that does not change shape when it is moved. *A rock is a solid.*

source page 130
The place or thing that something comes from. *The sun is a source of heat and light.*

standard unit page 110
A unit of measure that is the same all over the world. *A meter is a standard unit.*

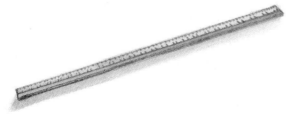

state of matter page 94
One of three forms that matter can take. *The three states of matter are solid, liquid, and gas.*

stomach page 214
An organ that changes food so the body can use it. *When you swallow food, it goes to your stomach.*

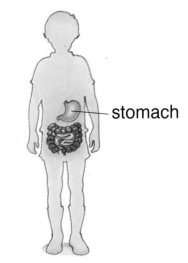

stomach

T

thunderstorm page 197
A storm that has wind, rain, lightning, and thunder. *The weather report said there were thunderstorms coming to our town.*

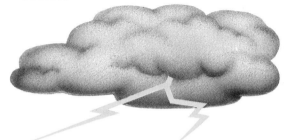

tornado page 198
A storm with fast, twisting winds that form a cloud that can touch the ground. *Tornadoes can harm buildings and trees.*

V

vaccine page 234
A shot or liquid given by a health-care worker to keep a person from getting an illness. *My doctor tells me when I need to have vaccines.*

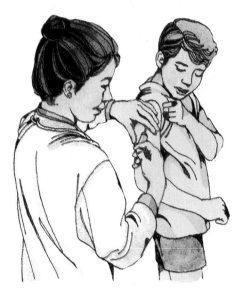

volume page 90
The amount of space something takes up. *A house has more volume than a box.*

W

water vapor page 103
The name given to water when it is a gas. *There is water vapor in the air.*

weather page 186
What the outside air is like. *Weather can be windy, rainy, sunny, hot, or cold.*

weather satellite page 202
An object made by people that circles the earth and sends back pictures about the weather. *We saw pictures taken by a weather satellite on the television weather report.*

wind page 188
Moving air. *You will need wind to fly the kite.*

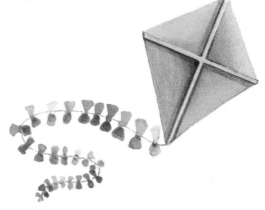

X
X ray page 240
A picture of the inside of the body. *The dentist took an X ray of my front tooth.*

Acknowledgements

Illustration Acknowledgements

Barbara Hoopes Ambler 50, 56, 57
Carl Dennis Buell 16, 17, 18, 19, 20, 21, 23, 26-27, 28-29, 30-31, 33, 36, 38, 43, 90, 245, 246L, 249L, 251TL
Larry Hughston 130, 168, 171, 173, 178, 180
Heather King 244, 246R, 249R, 250, 251BL, 253
Susan Jaekel 210, 211, 212, 214, 215, 219T, 247L, 248L
Lois Lovejoy 46, 66, 74, 222
Diana Magnuson 251TR, 252L
Deborah Morse 59, 102, 104, 110, 111, 112, 113, 114, 142, 170, 187, 232, 251TR, 252L
Sharron O'Neil 156, 158, 160, 186, 247R
Pronk & Associates / Paul Rivoche 120
Publisher's Graphics / Helen Davies 127
Publisher's Graphics / Marie De John 147, 165, 193
Publisher's Graphics / Pamela Johnson 53, 81, 107, 117, 139, 175, 183, 201, 219B, 229
Steven Schindler 63, 71, 99, 239
Carla Simmons 67

Photo Acknowledgements

4B Tim Davis*; 4CB Tom Walker/Stock, Boston; 4CT Chuck Fishman/Woodfin Camp & Associates; 4T Charles J. Alsheimer/Natural Selection; 6LB Robert C. Simpson/Tom Stack & Associates; 6LT Lois Moulton/Click-Chicago; 6R Jack D. Swenson/Tom Stack & Associates; 7B Mike Price/Bruce Coleman Inc.; 7T Fredrik D. Bodin/Stock, Boston; 8 Tim Davis*; 9 Tim Davis*; 12 Charles J. Alsheimer/Natural Selection

Lesson 1: 14 Sam Abell; 16 Lowell Georgia/Photo Researchers, Inc.; 17 Tom Bean/The Stock Market

Lesson 2: 24 © The Walt Disney Company; 25 Tim Davis*

Lesson 3: 34 Kevin Schafer/Tom Stack & Associates; 35 Tim Davis*; 36 Joe & Carol McDonald/Tom Stack & Associates; 37 Peter Vandermark/Stock, Boston; 39BR © Frans Lanting; 39L Robert Jureit/The Stock Market; 39TR Ray Richardson/Animals, Animals; 40 George B. Schaller; 41 © Ron Kimball

Lesson 4: 44 Steve Elmore/The Stock Market; 47 Breck P. Kent/Earth Scenes; 48T Tim Davis*; 49 Pat Lanza Field/Bruce Coleman Inc.; 51 Grant Heilman Photography

Lesson 5: 54 Patti Murray/Earth Scenes; 56 Steve Hansen/Stock, Boston; 58 C. McNulty/Click-Chicago; 59BC Zig Leszczynski/Earth Scenes; 59BL Dahlgren/The Stock Market; 59BR Patti Murray/Earth Scenes; 59TL Breck P. Kent/Earth Scenes; 59TR Milton Rand/Tom Stack & Associates; 60R Jon Feingersh/Click-Chicago

Lesson 6: 64 Patti Murray/Earth Scenes; 66BL Wardene Weisser/Bruce Coleman Inc.; 66BR John Gerlach/Click-Chicago; 66T Lynn M. Stone/Earth Scenes; 69BL B.G. Murray, Jr./Earth Scenes; 69BR Breck Kent/Earth Scenes; 69CL Dr. E.R. Degginger; 69CR Doug Sokell/Tom Stack & Associates; 69TL Rod Planck/Click-Chicago; 69TR Jack Wilburn/Earth Scenes

Lesson 7: 72 Patti Murray/Earth Scenes; 74 C. McNulty/Click-Chicago; 75 Dr. E.R. Degginger; 76BL Grant Heilman/Grant Heilman Photography; 76BR Runk-Schoenberger/Grant Heilman; 76TC Grant Heilman/Grant Heilman Photography; 76TL Runk-Schoenberger/Grant Heilman Photography; 76TR Runk-Schoenberger/Grant Heilman Photography; 77TL S. Rannels/Grant Heilman Photography; 77TR Grant Heilman/Grant Heilman Photography; 78 Kevin Schafer/Tom Stack & Associates; 79L J.H. Carmichael, Jr./Bruce Coleman Inc.; 81 Mike Mazzaschi/Stock, Boston; 82 Grant Heilman/Grant Heilman Photography; 83C,R Grant Heilman Photography; 83L Runk-Schoenberger/Grant Heilman Photography; 85 Leo Touchet*; 86 Chuck Fishman/Woodfin Camp & Associates

Lesson 8: 88 Spencer Swanger/Tom Stack & Associates; 89 Rick Browne ; 90B Mike Yamashita/Woodfin Camp & Associates; 90TL Oxford Scientific Films/Animals, Animals; 91 Janice Sheldon*; 92 Rick Browne*; 93 Rick Browne*; 95BL Tim Davis*; 95BR Rick Browne*; 96R Rick Browne*; 97BR Brian Parker/Tom Stack & Associates; 97T Stephen Frisch*; 98 Rick Browne*

Lesson 9: 100 Ken Lewis/Earth Scenes; 101 Rick Browne*; 102 Dr. E.R. Degginger; 103B Rod Planck/Tom Stack & Associates; 103T Stephen Frisch*; 104L Mark Tuschman*; 105T Richard Howard; 106 Rick Browne*

Lesson 10: 108 Tim Davis*; 109 Nick Pavloff*; 110 Nick Pavloff*; 111B Ken Sherman/Bruce Coleman Inc.; 111T Wendy Neefus/Earth Scenes; 112B Nick Pavloff*; 115B W.K. Almond/Stock, Boston; 115TL Robert Pearcy/Animals, Animals; 115TR Nick Pavloff*; 116 Nick Pavloff*

Lesson 11: 118 © Harald Sund

Lesson 12: 128 Thomas Kitchin/Tom Stack & Associates; 130 Breck Kent/Earth Scenes; 131B Stouffer Enterprises/Animals, Animals; 131TL Mark E. Gibson/The Stock Market; 131TR Bradley Olman/Bruce Coleman Inc.; 132B David M. Doody/Tom Stack & Associates; 132L Brian Parker/Tom Stack & Associates; 133BL Peter Menzel/Stock, Boston; 133BR Roy Morsch/The Stock Market; 133TL Rona Photography/Bruce Coleman Inc.; 133TR Mike Mazzaschi/Stock, Boston; 134 Richard Megna/Fundamental Photographs; 135B Tom Myers; 136B Bruce Davidson/Animals, Animals; 136T Elliott Smith*; 137B Robert Semeniuk/The Stock Market; 137C Chris Jones/The Stock Market; 137TL Ted Horowitz/The Stock Market; 137TR Miriam White/The Stock Market

Lesson 13: 140 Dr. Georg Gerster/Photo Researchers; 144 Mark Tuschman*; 147 Tim Davis*; 148 Chuck O'Rear/Woodfin Camp & Associates; 149L Dr. E.R. Degginger; 149R Mel Digiacomo/The Image Bank; 151L NASA; 151R Elliott Smith*; 152 Tom Walker/Stock, Boston

Lesson 14: 154 Scott Blackman/Tom Stack & Associates; 156BL Breck P. Kent/Earth Scenes; 156BR Grant Heilman Photography; 156TL Don & Pat Valenti/Tom Stack & Associates; 156TR Breck P. Kent/Earth Scenes; 157 Wendell Metzen/Bruce Coleman Inc.; 158B Robert McKenzie/Tom Stack & Associates; 158T Tony Arruza/ Bruce Coleman Inc.; 159BC Robert M. Friedman/Frozen Images; 159BL Wendy Neefus/Animals, Animals; 159BR Mike Mazzaschi/Stock, Boston; 159T Carl F. Roessler; 160R Roy Morsch/The Stock Market; 161BL Ed Hille/The Stock Market; 161BR Lee Foster/Bruce Coleman Inc.; 161TL Gabe Palmer/The Stock Market; 161TR Neal & Mary Jane Mishler; 162 James Karales/Peter Arnold, Inc.; 163L Ted Horowitz/The Stock Market; 163RB Sharon Cummings/ M.L. Dembinsky Associates

Lesson 15: 166 NASA; 168 R. Alan Bennington/The Stock Market; 170 Tim Davis*; 172B NASA; 172T Richard Megna/Fundamental Photographs; 174 Tim Davis*

Lesson 16: 176 Dr. E.R. Degginger; 177 Rick Browne*; 178L NASA; 178R NASA; 179B NASA; 179T NASA; 180 Lick Observatory/Univ. of California, Santa Cruz; 181 Richard Megna/Fundamental Photographs; 182 Rick Browne*

Lesson 17: 184 Elliott Smith*; 186 E.R. Degginger/Earth Scenes; 188C Mark E. Gibson/The Stock Market; 188L J. Sapinsky/The Stock Market; 189B Richard Buettner/Bruce Coleman Inc.; 189T © Jerry Jones; 190B Tom Pantages; 190T David Madison/Bruce Coleman Inc.; 191B C.C. Lockwood/Animals, Animals; 191T Gary Milburn/Tom Stack & Associates

Lesson 18: 194 © Tom Ives; 196BL Larry Lefever/Grant Heilman Photography; 196BR Grant Heilman Photography; 196T Scott Blackman/Tom Stack & Associates; 197B © David Madison; 197T Arjen Verkaik/The Stock Market; 198L E.R. Degginger/Earth Scenes; 198R NASA; 199 Rick Browne; 202 NASA; 203 Bill Gallery/Stock, Boston; 205 Lawrence Holl; 206 Tim Davis*

Lesson 19: 208 © David Madison; 209 Nick Pavloff*; 210 Nick Pavloff*; 212 Nick Pavloff*; 213L Charles Gupton/The Stock Market; 213RB © David Madison; 213RT © David Madison; 214 Sandy Roessler/The Stock Market; 215BL Victoria Beller-Smith/E.R. Degginger; 215BR Richard Thom/Tom Stack & Associates; 215TL © Elliott Smith; 215TR Pat Lanza Field/Bruce Coleman Inc.; 216B Nick Pavloff*; 216T Pete Saloutos/Click-Chicago; 217B Daemmrich/The Stock Market; 217T © David Madison; 218 Nick Pavloff*

Lesson 20: 220 Nick Pavloff*; 221 Nick Pavloff*; 222BL Philip Jon Bailey/Stock, Boston; 222BR Harry Hartman/Bruce Coleman Inc.; 222T James W. Kay/Bruce Coleman Inc.; 223B Nick Pavloff*; 223C Roy Morsch/The Stock Market; 223T Tom Stack/Tom Stack & Associates; 224C,R Elliott Smith*; 224L Nick Pavloff*; 225B Gabe Palmer/The Stock Market; 225TL Peter Vandai/The Stock Market; 225TR Paul Barton/The Stock Market; 226-7 Stephen Frisch*; 228 Nick Pavloff*

Lesson 21: 230 Gabe Palmer/The Stock Market; 231 Nick Pavloff*; 232 Elliott Smith*; 233 Elliott Smith*; 234B Elliott Smith*; 234T Michael Melford/The Image Bank; 235 Elliott Smith*; 236 Elliott Smith*; 237 Elliott Smith*; 238 Elliott Smith*; 240L Stuart L. Craig, Jr./Bruce Coleman Inc.; 240R David M. Doody/Tom Stack & Associates; 241L Warren Faubel/Bruce Coleman Inc.; 241R Howard Sochurek/Woodfin Camp & Associates; 243 Carol Palmer*

Wayland Lee*/Addison-Wesley Publishing Company: 48B, 60L, 61, 68 77B, 79R, 90TR, 94, 95T, 96L, 97BL, 104R, 105B, 112T, 113, 114, 122T, 124, 125T, 160L, 188R

All other photographs taken expressly for the publisher by Cindy Charles.

Front Cover: © Art Wolfe
Back Cover: Wayne Lynch/DRK Photo

*Photographs taken expressly for the publisher

Special thanks to: Alvarado Elementary School, San Francisco, CA; Buena Vista Annex, San Francisco, CA; Kathryn Burke School, San Francisco, CA; Crocker Highlands Elementary School, Oakland, CA; Live Oak School, San Francisco, CA; Peralta Year-Around Elementary School, Oakland, CA; Rising Star School, Alameda, CA; Selby Lane School, Redwood City, CA; Harry Slonaker Elementary School, San Jose, CA; University Heights Children's Center, Menlo Park, CA; Charles A. Whitten School, Oakland, CA; Willow Oaks School, Palo Alto, CA; YMCA Stonestown Summer School Program, San Francisco, CA; Olivia Stewart; University of California at Berkeley Astronomy Department; Tasha; The Nature Company, Stanford, CA.